CAMBRIDGE

FUN Skills

Student's Book 6

Stephanie Dimond-Bayir • Bridget Kelly

Cambridge University Press
www.cambridge.org/elt

Cambridge Assessment English
www.cambridgeenglish.org

Information on this title: www.cambridge.org/9781108563680

© Cambridge University Press and Cambridge Assessment 2020

First published 2020

20 19 18 17 16 15 14 13 12 11 10 9

Printed in Malaysia by Vivar Printing

A catalogue record for this publication is available from the British Library

ISBN 978-1-108-56368-0 Student's Book and Home Booklet with Online Activities

Contents

Map of the book

Unit	Topic	Skills focus	Can do	
1 Team time! page 6	Teamwork	**Speaking** Answer basic personal questions **Listening** Listen for words and colours Colour and write	Talk briefly about self Understand simple spoken descriptions	Think Big
2 Around the house page 10	Household objects	**Reading and Writing** Match descriptions to objects **Speaking** Understand statements, look at pictures and respond with differences	Match descriptions to objects Understand simple spoken descriptions Give simple descriptions of objects, pictures and actions	
Review Units 1–2 *page 14*				
3 Cool clubs page 16	Hobbies and leisure	**Listening** Listen for names, spelling and numbers Complete notes **Reading and Writing** Read and complete a dialogue	Understand simple spoken descriptions Read and understand short dialogues	
4 All about animals page 20	Animals	**Speaking** Respond to questions with short answers Answer questions about people/objects **Reading and Writing** Read for gist and specific information Complete gapped text	Understand and answer simple questions Ask simple questions Understand a short factual text	
Review Units 3–4 *page 24*				
5 Our perfect picnic page 26	Food	**Reading and Writing** Read a text and choose missing words to fill gaps **Speaking** Tell a story	Understand and complete a short factual text Understand a simple short story Tell a simple short story using pictures or own ideas	
6 In the jungle page 30	Wild animals and their environments	**Reading and Writing** Write a simple story **Listening** Listen for words, names and detailed information Match pictures and words	Write a short simple story using pictures or own ideas Understand simple spoken descriptions of objects, people or events	Think Big
Review Units 5–6 *page 34*				

Unit	Topic	Skills focus	Can do	
7 Planning a holiday page 36	Holidays	**Listening** Listen for specific information Tick the correct picture **Speaking** Understand the beginning of a story and continue	Understand simple spoken descriptions Understand simple short stories Tell a simple short story using pictures or own ideas	
8 I want to be a firefighter! page 40	Jobs	**Reading and Writing** Read and understand a short story Complete a text by selecting and copying the correct words in gaps. Complete a gapped text with one, two, three or four words	Read and understand simple stories	
Review Units 7–8 *page 44*				
9 Famous faces page 46	Celebrities	**Listening** Understand descriptions and match to pictures Answer personal questions.	Understand simple descriptions	
10 Let's go to space! page 50	Space	**Reading and Writing** Read and understand a short story Complete a gapped text with one, two, three or four words	Read and understand simple stories	Song
Review Units 9–10 *page 54*				
11 The Winter Olympics page 56	The Olympic Games	**Reading and Writing** Read and understand a text Complete a gapped text	Read and understand a short text	
12 Comics! page 60	Comic strips	**Reading and Writing** Write a story based on pictures	Write a short, simple story using pictures or own ideas	
Review Units 11–12 *page 64*				

Pairwork and song *pages 66–69*   **Skills checklists** *pages 78–81*

Grammar fun! *pages 70–75*   **Word list** *pages 82–85*

Grammar fun pairwork! *pages 76–77*   **Meet the characters** *pages 86–87*

1 Team time!

North Road School *Teams*

1 ___gym___ team

Do you love moving? Why not join our team and jump, dance and move your body? Come with us and dance in exciting competitions. Get stronger and make new friends at the same time.

We practise on Mondays at 5 pm and go to competitions at the weekends.

2 _____ team

Do you think about numbers every morning, afternoon and night? Do you dream of thousands and millions? Then join our team and make some new friends! Come to interesting competitions with us and win lots of prizes!

We practise number puzzles on Thursdays at 1 pm. We go to competitions once a month.

3 _____ team

Do you hate being inside all day? Are you interested in the environment? Then why not come and help us? We meet two lunchtimes a week and work hard to grow amazing plants that win prizes. Last year we won a prize in a fruit competition for growing a really big watermelon!

We meet on Tuesdays and Thursdays at 1 pm. The fruit and vegetable competitions are usually in the summer.

4 _____ team

Are you interested in taking photographs and learning how to paint pictures? Do you love drawing things and choosing colours? Then come and have fun with cameras and paint. Make beautiful posters and take amazing photographs to win competitions.

We meet on Wednesdays at 5 pm. We always have a 'best-picture-of-the-week' competition that you can join.

1 👁 **Look, read and label the school teams.**

maths   gardening   ~~gym~~   art

2 🔊 02 **Read the texts again and listen to the school children. Which team can they join? Then complete the sentences.**

1 **Helen Jones 12** _____
Helen wants to get stronger and _____.

2 **Harry Lane 11** _____
Harry likes drawing and he's good at _____.

3  **Sophia Price 10** _____
Sophia _____ and isn't busy on Mondays.

4 **Aziz Patel 11** _____
Aziz wants to learn something new. He's _____ growing plants.

3 💬 **Which team would you like to join? Tell a friend.**

I'd like to join the maths team.

Why?

Because I love numbers and puzzles. And you? Which team would you like to join?

4 **Complete the questions using the correct form of the verbs in brackets.**

1 Are you good at _____making_____ (make) food?

2 Do you dream of _____ (win) a big chess competition?

3 Do you hate _____ (sit) on a chair all day?

4 Are you interested in _____ (learn) a new sport like ice skating and winning prizes?

5 💬 **Work with a friend. Match these answers to questions in task 4. Then give each team a name.**

☐ **A** Join our team and make new friends! Learn everything you need to know to dance on frozen water! Try to win first prize in the winter sports competition.

_____

☐ **B** Why not join our team? We have lots of great players for you to practise with. We enjoy playing other board games, too!

_____

1 **C** Join the school cooking team and learn to cook delicious meals for you and your friends. Next year, we're going to cook a meal in a competition on TV! Can you help us win?

_____

☐ **D** Why not join our running team and get moving fast? We often race other school teams and we win lots of prizes.

_____

6 **Look at the flags. Which teams A–D in task 5 are they for?**

THINK BIG

Why join a team?
- you get free drinks and snacks
- you get out of the house more
- you're not alone

What else?

Which team?

1 🔊 03 **Listen and complete the table for Helen.**

Name	Surname	Age	Team	Why would you like to join the team?	What are you good at?
Helen	Jones	12			

2 💬 **Ask and answer with a friend. Make a table that is true for you and your friend using task 1 as an example.**

> Hi Peter! What's your surname and how old are you?

> My surname's ... and I'm ...

> Which team would you like to join?

> I'd like to join the ... team, because I like ... and I'm good at ...

3 🔊 04 **Look at the flags. Listen and colour. Then write a name for the team.**

1 _____

2 _____

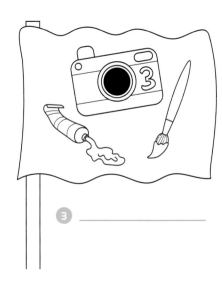

3 _____

4 🔊 05 Listen and colour and write. There is one example.

POND

GARDEN

1 **06** **Listen to the children. Circle the differences they talk about.**

2 💬 Find six more differences. Tell a friend. Did you find the same differences?

> In this picture there's a ... / the ... is eating / taking / playing / wearing ...

> In this picture, the ... is ... / he's / she's eating / taking / playing / wearing ...

3 Look at the words around the box in task 4. Match the words to the places in the box.

kitchen   bathroom   your bag   outside

4 ✏️ Look and read the sentences. Write the correct words on the lines. There is one example.

shampoo

towel

combs

telephone

toothbrush

soap

diary

shelves

stamps

cushions

~~fridge~~

gate

swings

oven

key

You can put food like milk and butter in here to keep them cold.   *fridge*

1   You can use it to open a door. It's quite small and made of metal.   _____

2   People put these on envelopes, when they post letters.   _____

3   You can use this to cook food. You make bread and cakes in it.   _____

4   People clean their teeth with this.   _____

5   You use this to speak to someone who is in another place.   _____

6   This is a book where you can write about your day and your ideas.   _____

7   You use it to wash your hair.   _____

8   Children have fun on these in the park!   _____

9   These are soft and people put them on chairs to sit on.   _____

10   These are long pieces of wood or plastic on the wall. People put things like cups, books or photos on them.   _____

TIP! Be careful when you copy a word. Check if it is plural.

5 ✏️ Circle the four words that you did not use. Choose one and write a sentence about it. Show a friend. Can they guess what it is?

1 Look at the words in the box, then write them on the correct line.

~~China~~   wood   USA   Italy   cook   king   brick   stone   queen   metal

Country: _China_

Made of: _____

Person: _____

2 🔊 07 Listen and number the photos.

A

B

C

3,000 *years*

How old?		How old?		How old?	
Where from?		Where from?		Where from?	
Made of?		Made of?		Made of?	
Who used it?		Who used it?		Who used it?	
What for?		What for?		What for?	

3 🔊 07 Listen again and complete the information for each photo.

4 💬 Ask and answer with a friend.

Which thing is the oldest / the most beautiful / the most interesting?

I think the ... is the oldest / the most beautiful / the most interesting because ...

5 💬 Look at the armchairs. Where do you think they are? Who do you think lives there? Make notes and tell the class.

> We think A is in an old house in the countryside. A farmer lives there. She likes reading.

6 👁 Read the story about an armchair quickly and tick (✓) the correct photo. Read again and complete the text.

The story of our armchair

This armchair is the oldest thing in our 1 *home* . It's about 70 years old and it 2 _____ from Italy. It's in the living room and it's made of 3 _____ and blue leather. My grandmother uses it to watch TV, sit and 4 _____ the newspaper. She bought it when she was 20 years 5 _____ .

7 ✏ Choose one of the other armchairs from task 5 to complete the table. Use your own ideas.

- How old?
- Where from?
- Where is it now?
- Made of?
- Who uses it?
- What do they use it for?
- Some more information

8 Write the story of this armchair in about 50 words.

Skills: Listening and Speaking

1 🔊 **08** **Which competition did they enter? Listen and write the names under the photos. There is one extra name.**

> Betty   Robert   Sarah   Alice   Holly

1. _____

2. _____

3. _____

4. _____Betty_____

Mark: ___ / 3

2 🔊 **08** **Listen again and write T (true) or F (false).**

1 Betty won the competition that she entered. _____

2 Betty got a horse for her birthday. _____

3 Alice went to a competition by the sea. _____

4 Alice's uncle came to watch her in the competition. _____

5 Robert is not very good at sport. _____

6 Sarah's team won a big box of strawberries last weekend. _____

Mark: ___ / 6

3 **Can you correct the false sentences? Try to remember and tell a friend.**

> Betty got a ... for her birthday.

Mark: ___ / 4

Total: ___ / 13

Skills: Reading and Writing

1 **Read and complete the sentences with the correct words.**

restaurant   comb   telephone   stone   metal   oven

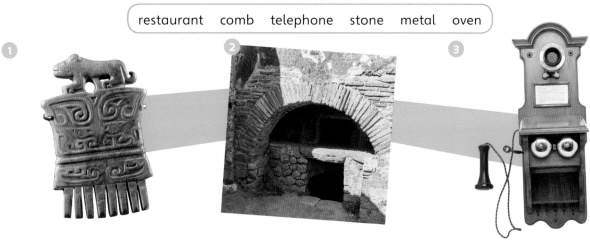

This **1** _____ is about 3,000 years old. It's made of a beautiful, brown **2** _____ and it comes from China. A rich person, like a king or queen, used it to tidy their hair.

You can see this **3** _____ in Italy. It's almost 2,000 years old. It's made of bricks. A cook used it to make bread to sell to people in a **4** _____ .

This **5** _____ is made of wood and **6** _____ and it's called a 'wall telephone'. It's about 120 years old and it's from the USA.

Mark: ___ / 6

2 **Look at the picture and write about six things that you can see.**

1 _There's some honey on the shelf._
2 _The woman is eating pizza._

Mark: ___ / 12

Total: _____ / 18

CHECKLIST

☐ I used capital letters and full stops.

☐ I checked my spelling.

☐ My handwriting is clear.

3 Cool clubs

To Frank

Hi Frank!

How are you? I'm fine.
I went to Adventure Club
yesterday and it is really cool –
we do a lot of different games and sports
and try new hobbies. I'm not very good at
some of them, but I have a lot of fun and I
am getting braver every week. Last week
I climbed to the top of a special climbing
wall and I was so happy. But games are my
favourite because I like to try out different
games. I played chess last week. It was
really interesting, but it sounded horrible!
Shall we start a club too?

Love Sophia ☺

1 **What does Sophia enjoy doing most at Adventure Club?
Tick (✓) the box next to the correct photo A–E.**

2 1 **Look at the photos of things she does at the club. Find the words in the puzzle.**

skateboardingswimmingclimbingchessplayingvolleyball

2 **Say the club activities and point to the photos in task 1.**

3 **Sophia and Frank are thinking about different types of club they can start. Complete the table with the words from the box.**

design   rocket   geography   business   drum

1	We draw pictures of things we want to make or houses we want to live in.	*design*	club
2	We learn about different countries, climate change and how the environment works.		club
3	We are noisy but we have fun! Our music is great.		club
4	We think of ideas to make money and we learn how to plan well.		club
5	We find out about space and what astronauts do.		club

4 **Which club from task 3 is best for these things? Why? There may be more than one answer. Talk to a friend.**

1 Using your body
2 Working in a team
3 Making friends
4 Finding answers to problems
5 Learning how to plan

5 🔊 09 **Listen. What kind of club do Sophia and Frank choose?**

6 🔊 09 **Listen again and write. There is one example.**

A new club

1	They will learn:	about different _countries_ .
2	Name of club:	the _____ club
3	Time of meeting:	_____ on Fridays
4	Place of meeting:	room _____
5	People will bring:	a _____ to the first meeting.

TIP! Make sure you know the letters of the alphabet in English.

7 ✏️ **Work with a friend. Choose one of the clubs from page 16 and complete the table.**

Name of the club:	
What you will do:	
Time of the club:	
Place:	
What to bring?	

8 💬 **Talk to another friend. Ask questions about their club and tell them about your club.**

What's the name of your club?

It's called Drum Crazy!

Where is it?

It's on the sports field so no one can hear!

1 🔊 **10** Listen to the first part of the story. What does each person want to do? Write a name under each photo. Use one name twice.

Emma   Harry   Richard

1 _____   2 _____   3 _____   4 _____

2 🔊 **11** Listen to the second part of the story. Why were Emma, Harry and Richard the best in the circus show? Read some of the story in the poster below.

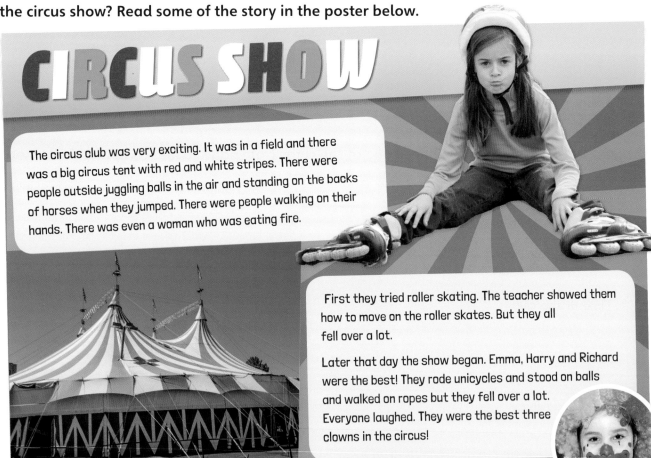

CIRCUS SHOW

The circus club was very exciting. It was in a field and there was a big circus tent with red and white stripes. There were people outside juggling balls in the air and standing on the backs of horses when they jumped. There were people walking on their hands. There was even a woman who was eating fire.

First they tried roller skating. The teacher showed them how to move on the roller skates. But they all fell over a lot.

Later that day the show began. Emma, Harry and Richard were the best! They rode unicycles and stood on balls and walked on ropes but they fell over a lot. Everyone laughed. They were the best three clowns in the circus!

3 🔊 **12** Listen again. What did they say? Match the sentences. Now listen and check.

1 We should join the circus club.
2 Ouch!
3 I'm not doing that in the air!
4 This is terrible.
5 It's OK.

A That hurts!
B It's too dangerous!
C I have an idea.
D A circus club? That sounds amazing!
E What are we going to do in the show?

4 🔊 13 **Read and listen to the dialogue between Sophia and Frank. Draw lines between the sentences.**

 SOPHIA

 FRANK

1 How are you? ——————— Yes, I am. It's going to be great!

2 What time shall we meet? There are quite a lot. I think about 14.

3 Where is it? Let's go at five o'clock.

4 How many people are coming? In room 11.

5 Are you excited? I'm OK, thanks. Just a bit tired.

---

5 👁 **Sophia is asking Frank some questions about the next club meeting. Read the conversation. Write a letter A–H for Frank's answer.**

1 **Sophia:** We had a great first meeting, didn't we?

   Frank: _C_

2 **Sophia:** When shall we have the next one?

   Frank: ____

3 **Sophia:** Do you want to talk about volcanoes?

   Frank: ____

4 **Sophia:** What do we need to prepare?

   Frank: ____

5 **Sophia:** Shall we take some food and drinks again?

   Frank: ____

6 **Sophia:** Where shall we meet?

   Frank: ____

A Yes, I'll talk about them and show some pictures.

B I think we can use room 6A this time.

C *Yes, it was amazing!* **(example)**

D OK. But you did it last time, so I'll bring some fruit and biscuits this time.

E No, we can't.

F Let's meet next Wednesday at the same time.

G We should get some pictures of volcanoes.

H I didn't go there.

---

6 💬 **Talk about your own club with a friend. Ask and answer questions.**

4 All about animals

ANIMAL  WORLD

Insect World   Big Beast World   Small Beast World   Bird World   Sea World

Welcome to Animal World, the best website to find out about different kinds of creatures!

1 💬 Look at the website about animals. Where can you find information about each one? Use the five tabs to help you. Ask and answer questions.

What's this animal?

It's an eagle.

Where's it from?

It's from Bird World, of course!

2 ✏️ Look at the numbers. Make sentences using a number and an animal from the website in task 1.

2   3   8   40

Example: _____ *2 – A swan has two wings!*

3 🔊14 Betty is visiting a wildlife park with her father. Listen and write numbers.

1 An octopus has _____ arms.

2 An octopus lives for about _____ years.

3 An eagle can see for _____ miles.

4 There are nearly _____ thousand kinds of spider.

4 **Look at the picture and read the sentences. Write the animals' names on the signs.**

1 The penguins have got a pond in their home near the café. There's a man with a hat watching them.

2 The camels are opposite the penguins. They've got sand, lots of trees and some pyramids.

3 The beetles are in the insect cage next to the home for the camels. There is a small girl looking at them through the glass window.

4 The octopus is in an aquarium near the café. There is a boy with binoculars looking for the octopus.

5 The eagles are sitting in trees near the café. They are high up.

Food chains

1 💬 **Work with a friend. Look at the information about two animals.**
Ask and answer questions and complete the information.
Student A's information about two animals is below.
Student B's information about two animals is on page 66.

	Penguins	Camels
Like eating	Fish	Grass and plants
Where	On the ice in cold places	In the desert
Dangerous for people?	No	Not usually

Like eating		
Where		
Dangerous for people?		

2 **Work with a friend. Look at the photos. What animal is it? What do you think it eats? Use**
might.

Photo A might be a giraffe.
It might eat leaves.

I think giraffes eat plants.
They might eat leaves from
trees too.

3 👁 ✏️ **Read the text. Choose a word from the box. Write the correct word next to numbers 1–5. There is one example. Then write the correct animal name A-D to complete the food chain.**

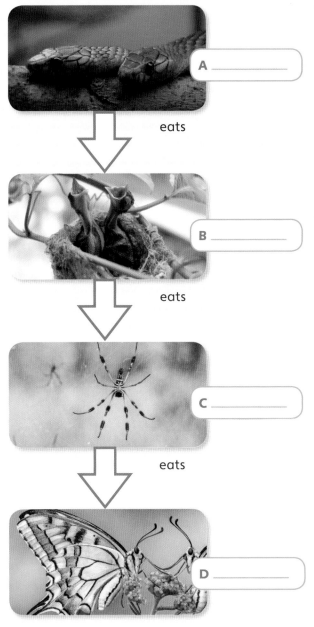

A _____

eats

B _____

eats

C _____

eats

D _____

> ~~vegetables~~ corners nests view extinct
> empty problem top important leaf

Animals all need food to live. Some animals only eat **0** _vegetables_ and plants. Others eat meat.

A food chain shows us what different animals eat. For example, some snakes catch and eat birds or take eggs from their **1** _____ . Birds eat insects and spiders – they can see them from far away and fly down to catch them. Spiders often catch butterflies and flying insects in their webs. But butterflies don't eat other creatures. They drink nectar, a kind of sugary water, from flowers and they eat other parts of plants.

The butterfly is below all the other animals in the food chain because it doesn't eat any of the other creatures. The snake is at the **2** _____ of the chain above the other animals.

Sometimes animals in the food chain become **3** _____ . This 'breaks' the food chain, which is a **4** _____ because some animals don't have enough of the food they usually eat. They have to find other food. So all the different animals are **5** _____ parts of the food chain.

4 **Now choose the best name for the text. Tick (✓) the box.**

Insects love flying ☐

Food chains ☐

Flowers and plants ☐

Review Unit 3

Skills: Writing and Speaking

1 Richard goes to university. He studies a lot now. But he had a lot of hobbies when he was 12 years old. Look at the picture of his room. What two instruments and two sports did he like?

2 Complete the sentences.

1 Richard liked music because _____

2 He enjoyed reading books about _____

3 He also liked reading _____

4 He played _____

5 He _____

Mark: ___ / 10

3 What hobbies do you have? Draw a picture and label it with 5 things to show your hobbies. Show your friend.

Mark: ___ / 5

4 Which types of club and verbs to do with clubs can you remember from Unit 3? Complete the table.

name of club	design
verbs about clubs	join

Mark: ___ / 5

Total: ___ ___ / 20

Skills: Reading and Speaking

1 **Find the words in the puzzle. Draw lines to the picture.**

F	S	O	O	C	T	O	P	U	S
E	W	C	C	A	I	C	W	E	P
B	U	T	T	E	R	F	L	Y	I
U	B	O	G	A	E	W	P	L	D
J	A	R	E	G	A	K	N	M	E
D	E	T	U	L	A	C	Y	Y	R
A	R	O	B	E	E	T	L	E	L
N	T	I	A	S	W	B	U	Y	E
E	O	S	W	A	N	T	U	W	P
L	A	E	Y	A	C	A	M	E	L

Mark: ____ / 8

2 **Look at the pictures of animals in task 1. Which animals:**

1 eat meat or other creatures?

2 only eat plants or grass?

3 live in a nest?

4 can get to the top of a tree?

Mark: ____ / 8

3 **Talk to a friend. Use with _might_ if you are not sure.**

> I think eagles eat meat because they catch small animals.

> Yes. But I'm not sure about camels. They might eat meat. Do you know?

4 **Work in small groups. Play a guessing game.**

> Do you build a nest?

> Yes.

> You might be a swan!

> No I'm not.

Mark: ____ / 4

Total: ____ / 20

25

5 Our perfect picnic

OLIVER

KATY

1 — sandwiches

1 Look at the photos of food in task 2.
Label photos 1–8 with words from the box.

> sandwiches chocolate strawberries yoghurt
> chicken and pasta salad biscuit jam pizza olives

2 15 **What foods are Katy and Oliver bringing
to their picnic? Listen and draw lines.**

3 Look at the food pyramid and Katy's and
Oliver's picnics in task 2. Then answer
the questions.

1 Who has something from every food group?

2 Who has the most food from the yellow food group?

3 Who has the most food from the red food group?

4 Who has the most fruit and vegetables?

5 Who do you think has a healthy picnic? Why?

> This food pyramid shows the five
> different food groups. It can help
> us to choose healthy foods to eat.

Food groups

We should only eat a little of these foods every day

We should only eat these foods two or three times a day

We should eat lots of these foods every day

4 **Read the text in task 5 and answer the questions.**

1 Why isn't eating sugar healthy?

2 How much sugar can we eat every day?

3 Which foods have sugar hiding in them?

4 What can we do to eat less sugar?

5 ✏️ **Choose the right words and write them on the lines. There is one example**

SUGAR

		much	many	few
0	Do you know how _much_ sugar you eat? It's more than you think.	(much)	many	few
1	Sugar is delicious and we _____ it in lots of different foods. We put it in cakes, biscuits, ice cream and some	used	uses	use
2	yoghurts to make _____ taste sweet. But eating a lot of	them	it	they
3	sugar isn't healthy. It can hurt _____ teeth and make us sick. So we shouldn't eat more than 25 grams of sugar every day. But there's a problem. There's also sugar in food which doesn't taste sweet. We can sometimes find sugar in bread,	ours	our	us
4	soup _____ even cheese. Some people	and	but	not
5	_____ add sugar to the tomato sauce on pizzas.	also	too	else
6	So, how can we _____ the quantity of sugar we are eating? One way is to read the bottles and boxes of the	know	knew	knows
7	food _____ we eat. They have information about how much sugar there is so we can choose healthy food. Another	what	that	who
8	way _____ eat less sugar, is to make our own bread, soup and pizza. Then we can add as little sugar as we like or	for	to	it
9	_____ at all. Of course, the best way to be healthy	no	none	not
10	is to stop eating _____ sweets, ice creams and cakes. But that's very difficult because they taste so good!	they	any	each

6 Choose six foods you would like to have for a picnic. Make a list. How much sugar do you think they have?

Picnic list	Sugar
1 piece of pizza	4g
1 chicken salad	3g
2 chocolate biscuits	7g
1 box of strawberries	3g
1 fruit yoghurt	10g
1 small bottle of lemonade	12g
Total:	39g!

1 **16** Listen to the first part of the story and write the names. Point and say where each child wants to eat.

Where shall we have our picnic?

a ruined castle

a cave in a forest

a sparkling stream with a grassy bank

a waterfall

Anna

~~Anna~~ Ben Alex Holly

2 💬 **17** Talk with a friend. Where do you think the children will eat their picnic? Now listen to the second part of the story and check your answer.

3 **17** Listen again to the second part and draw the correct food on the plates.

The fun picnic

A
Anna

B

C

D

4 💬 Look at the pictures again. The children wanted to have a picnic. On the bus, they talked about where to eat. Now you tell the story.

5 👁 **Read the invitation. Talk with a friend.**
Why is Eva having a picnic?

Subject: My picnic!

Hi Pedro,
Can you come to my 1 _birthday_ picnic? It's this Saturday afternoon by the lake. You can get there by bus or bike.
We'll have lots of 2 _____ food like rainbow fruit bowls, salads and of course a big birthday cake! You should bring some food too, but don't bring too many cookies or sweets. Let's be 3 _____ !
Bring your guitar and play us a song! And bring your swimsuit and an umbrella. It could be 4 _____ or rainy!
We'll have blankets to sit on, kites to fly if it's 5 _____ , footballs to kick and 6 _____ games to play. But don't forget to help me clean up at the end.
We should leave the lake as tidy as we find it.
See you there!
Eva

6 ✏ **Read the invitation again and write the correct word on the lines.**

delicious   sunny   healthy   funny   ~~birthday~~   windy

7 **Now use the information in the invitation to complete the table about Eva's picnic.**

	Eva	Your name
When		
Where		
Food		
Food not to bring		
What else to bring		
Things to do		
Don't forget to		

8 **Work in groups to plan your birthday picnic. Use the table to help you.**

9 ✏ **Write your invitation. Use some words about the weather, the food and having fun.**

6 In the jungle

1 lion

2

3

4

A B C D

1 Write the names of the animals then tell a partner.

beetle ~~lion~~ swan dinosaur

2 18 Match the footprints to the animals. Listen and check.

3 Read the magazine article about Janet. Does she enjoy her job?

Janet has a very unusual job. She works in a big nature park in Africa as a wild animal tracker. She knows what the footprints of different wild animals look like so that she can track or follow them and learn how to keep them safe.

Janet's job can be difficult. Sometimes it's very hot and she has to walk for a long time to find the animals that she is tracking. She often follows the footprints of big animals like elephants. Elephants can walk hundreds of kilometres and they can be frightening when they are angry. Because of this, Janet doesn't usually work alone. She works with a team of trackers, who can help each other if an animal becomes dangerous.

Janet loves her job because she is very interested in wild animals and what they do every day. Her favourite animals are giraffes and lions. She thinks it's very important to look after the environment.

4 Can you remember what these adjectives describe? Cover the article and write a sentence for each adjective. Read the article again and check.

1 unusual   *Janet's job is unusual.*

2 safe   _____

3 difficult   _____

4 angry   _____

5 dangerous   _____

6 important   _____

5 Would you like to be a tracker? Why? / Why not? Tell a friend.

6 **Look at the three pictures and choose some words from the box to make notes about what happened in each picture.**

> forest   jungle   surprised   excited   enormous   large   dinosaur   follow   felt   thought
> tracker   guessed   fun   costume   chicken   was   cat   lion   found   friendly   special
> unusual   footprint(s)   boy   frightened   were   birthday party   followed

7 **Tell a friend what happened in the pictures. Circle the words in the box that your friend uses.**

8 ✏️ **Write about this story. Write 20 or more words.**

_____

_____

_____

_____

CHECKLIST

After you write, show your story to a friend. Tick (✓) the boxes.

☐ Is the spelling correct?

☐ Is the story more than 20 words?

☐ Does the story talk about all three pictures?

☐ Is the handwriting clear?

1 Look at the photos in task 3. Complete the table with the animals' names. Which animals have fur, wings, spots or a shell? Tick (✓) the correct box.

animal	fur	wings	spots	shell
0 *butterfly*		✓		
1				
2				
3				
4				
5				

2 🎧 19 Listen and answer the questions.

1 Why does Maria take photos? _____ 3 How long do tortoises live? _____

2 What do camels like eating? _____ 4 What are eagles good at? _____

3 🎧 19 Where did Maria take each of these photos? Look at the photos on page 33. Listen and write a letter in each box. There is one example.

0   G

1

2

3

4

5

TIP! Listen to the whole dialogue before you choose your answer.

4 👁 **Read the questions and match them to the answers.
What animal do you think it is? Draw a picture.**

1 Where's your home? _D_

2 What's your favourite food? ___

3 What are you frightened of? ___

4 Do you walk, swim or fly? ___

5 Have you got fur or a shell? ___

6 What are you good at? ___

7 What colour are you? ___

8 How long do you live? ___

A No, I haven't got those things but I have got wings.

B I usually fly and walk, but I can swim when I have to.

C Nothing, because I'm fast, strong and brave.

D I live in a nest in a tree.

E I can see things that are very far away. I can fly very quickly.

F Rabbits are delicious!

G Sometimes I can live for 50 years.

H I can be brown, white or black. I often have yellow eyes.

THINK BIG

Which animals help humans?

- transportation
- guide the blind
- company for the old

33

Skills: Writing and Speaking

1 Choose six foods that you would like to have in a picnic. Draw and label your picnic.

Mark: ___ / 6

2 Now look at your picnic and make notes.

1 Which food groups are in your picnic?

_____

2 Which foods in your picnic have sugar in them?

_____

3 Could you make your picnic healthier? How?

_____

Mark: ___ / 3

3 Find out about a friend's picnic and make notes in the table.

> What food is in your picnic?

> There are cheese sandwiches, tomatoes and …

Find out about …	My friend's picnic
the food in his or her picnic.	
the food groups in his or her picnic.	
the foods with sugar in his or her picnic.	
how his or her picnic could be healthier.	

Mark: ___ / 8

4 What else are you going to take to your picnic? Write three things. Tell your friend.

> I'm also going to take an umbrella to my picnic.

umbrella _____ _____ _____

Mark: ___ / 3

Total: ___ ___ / 20

Skills: Listening and Reading

1 🔊 **20** **Listen to Harry talking about his pets and complete the sentences.**

1 Harry would really like to have a pet _____ .

2 Harry has two pets: a _____ and a _____ .

3 Their skin is cold and _____ – a bit like a dinosaur.

4 Harry has to keep his pets _____ .

5 Harry's friends think his pets are _____ .

Mark: ___ / 6

2 **What's wrong? Read, think and remember what Harry said.**
Can you correct the words in red?

books

Harry has lots of **0** ~~DVDs~~ about dinosaurs. There **1** are lots of dinosaurs living

now. Harry's **2** brother said, 'How about getting a pet that **3** *sounds like* a dinosaur

instead?' Harry thought that was a great idea so he did some **4** running and he

decided to get a pet lizard and a pet tortoise. They both look a bit like a dinosaur

because they don't have **5** feet. Harry's **6** dinosaur is called Fred and he's quite

small. His tortoise is bigger and she's called Pat. Lizards often live in **7** lakes and

tortoises often live in **8** nests. Fred and Pat like eating fruit and cheese. Harry feeds

them **9** five times a day. Harry thinks that Fred and Pat are **10** fun! They are very

11 dangerous and they are beautiful. Fred has **12** orange spots on his **13** legs and

Pat has brown stripes on her **14** head. They aren't dinosaurs but they are Harry's

perfect friends!

3 🔊 **20** **Listen to Harry again and**
check your answers.

Mark: ___ ___ / 14

Total: ___ ___ / 20

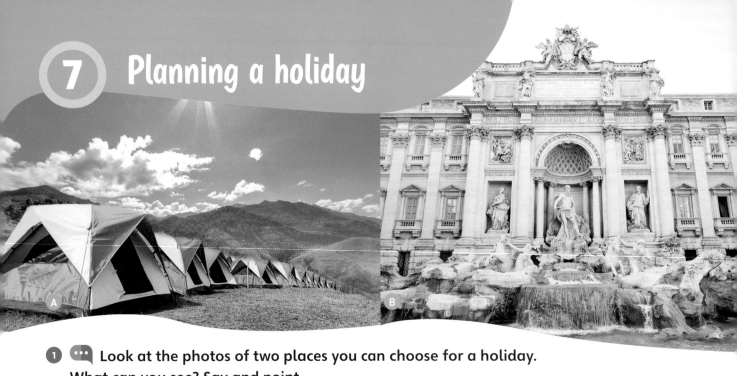

7 Planning a holiday

1 💬 **Look at the photos of two places you can choose for a holiday. What can you see? Say and point.**

> countryside   city centre   museum   mountains   tent   field   stone   grass   building   statue

2 **Photo A is in the South of France. Photo B is in Rome, Italy. In which place can you usually find these things? Write A or B.**

1 a police station _____
2 a bridge over a stream _____
3 a busy restaurant _____
4 a fire station _____

5 woods or forest _____
6 wild animals _____
7 a university _____
8 a farm _____

3 👁 **Read about Oliver and Sarah. Decide which place they might like best, A or B? Why? Tell a friend.**

Oliver is very quiet. He likes drawing and seeing old places. History is his favourite subject and he loves finding out about how people lived in different times. He is happy outside but he likes going into museums and castles and other places where he can learn about life in the past.

Sarah is very friendly. She likes meeting people and doing lots of sports. She has a lot of energy. She enjoys exploring new places especially outside. Last year she went on safari in South Africa and saw lots of wild animals.

4 **Oliver and Sarah are going on holiday with their mum and dad. Here is the list of their plans. Put the plans in the correct order.**

1   *Choose a place to go to.*
2 _____
3 _____
4 _____
5 _____
6 _____

- Pack your bags.
- Go to the airport or station and start your journey!
- Find out how to travel there (for example by plane/bus).
- Buy tickets.
- Check you have important things (your passport/currency) ready to pack.
- ~~Choose a place to go to.~~

5 Look at the photos. Write the words on the lines.

~~taxi~~ theatre museum plane desert tent skyscraper mountains
snowboarding ocean castle farm restaurant hotel

1
 A
 B
 C
 D

taxi _____   train   bus   _____

2
 A
 B
 C
 D

city   countryside   _____   _____

3
 A
 B
 C
D

_____   factory   _____   _____

4
A
B
 C
 D

_____   _____   _____   _____

5
A
B

 C
D

_____   _____   _____   swim at the beach

6 🔊21 Listen to Sarah and her grandfather talking about a holiday. Is Sarah going to France or Italy?

7 🔊21 Listen again. Which things hasn't Sarah done yet? Listen and tick (✓) the boxes in task 5.

8 ✏️ 💬 Write about you using the pictures from lines 1–5 in task 5.
Then tell a friend.

I'd like to travel by **1** _____ . I haven't been to **2** _____ before. I want to see

3 _____ . I'd like to visit **4** _____ and **5** _____ .

1 How do you say hello to someone new in your country? Tick (✓) the best photo.

a bow   **b** shake hands   **c** put your hands together   **d** smile   **e** something else?

2 👁 Holly went on holiday to visit her friend. Read about her trip and answer the questions.

1 Where did Holly go?

2 Did she enjoy the holiday?

3 Did Holly think culture shock was a good thing?

Holly's adventure in Malaysia

Last year Holly went to Malaysia to visit her friend Nur. 'You will have a great time,' said her mum. 'But you might feel some culture shock!'

'What's that?' said Holly.

'Well, our culture is the way we live – our food, our hobbies, our everyday life,' said her mum. 'But when you go somewhere very different, everything seems strange. So you can feel a bit worried or surprised.' So Holly read a lot about Malaysia and it helped.

For example, she knew that she could shake hands to say hello but she used two hands, not just one. Nur's mother and father were very pleased. 'You've learned about Malaysian culture!' they said. 'That's great!'

The first morning Nur gave her rice in banana leaves for breakfast. 'Rice!' said Holly. 'I read that you sometimes have rice for breakfast here. And now I'm trying it!' She was happy.

In the street Holly wasn't surprised when she couldn't read everything because the signs were in different languages. And her favourite part of the holiday was watching a special Malaysian dance and trying on a Malaysian dress.

When Holly got home her mother asked, 'Was Malaysia very different?' 'Yes,' said Holly. 'I loved Malaysia and I loved the culture shock. It wasn't too bad because I read about it before I went. I learned a lot about a different country. And I feel more confident now. I've learned I can do new things on my own!'

3 💬 Read the text again. Put the photos in the correct order.

4 💬 Draw another picture from the story in the last box. Show a friend. Can they guess which part of the story it is?

5 💬 Work with another friend. Tell the story again, using the photos.

6 💬 When Holly was in Malaysia she had an adventure. Look at the pictures below. What can you see?

7 Which words might go with each picture?

> train station   platform   forgot   friendly   remembered   worried   happy

Adventure in Malaysia

TIP! Say a few words about each picture. Use action verbs e.g. *come, go, buy, carry, lose, find*.

8 💬 Look at the pictures again. *Holly and Nur were going on a day trip. Holly had made a plan. They were going by train. At the station ... Now you tell the story.*

8 I want to be a firefighter!

What I want to do!

Welcome to my blog ... all the things I'm thinking and doing!

Example: Hi everyone. This week I'm thinking about jobs and what I want to do _____*in*_____ the future. Do you know

1 which job you might want to do one day?! It's really difficult to choose – there are _____ interesting jobs.

At school we're learning about different skills. Skills are things you can do well because you have practised

2 a lot or _____ them. For example, cooking is a useful skill because you can make yourself good food.

Yesterday, our teacher talked about two kinds of skills. Hard skills are things you learn at school like maths

3 and using a computer program. You probably need a teacher to help _____ . Soft skills are things like listening well or working in a team. We practise those skills at school but I also learn them at home, with my sister and brother. We have to do things together and learn to speak and listen to each other. It's good practice!

4 For most jobs you need some hard and soft skills. Mechanics needs to be good _____ fixing things and working with machines. But they also have to talk to people about problems, so they have to be good at speaking to people too.

5 When I'm older I want to be a firefighter. I think I _____ need to understand science and how fires happen. But I'm also good at speaking to people – I'll need to tell people what to do in a fire, so they are safe.

If you know the skills you do best, it might help you choose the type of job you want to do one day. Good luck!

Katy

---

1 👁 **Read Katy's blog about jobs. Answer the questions.**

1 What is she learning about at school this week?

2 Which hard skills does a mechanic need? Which soft skills?

2 **Read the blog again and write the correct words on the lines. There is one example.**

Example:	at	in	on		3 you	your	them
1 much	a lot of	none		**4** in	on	at
2 learn	learning	learned		**5** will	can	did

3 **Are these soft skills or hard skills? Look at the table and write the words from the box in the correct place.**

listening well   fixing machines   working in a team   speaking clearly   working hard
maths   using a computer   reading Italian   helping other people   understanding science

Hard skills

fixing machines

Soft skills

listening well

4 💬 **Choose a job. Which hard skills and which soft skills does this person need? Talk to a friend.**

> A doctor needs to be good at science. She or he needs to listen well and explain things clearly. She or he needs to be good at helping people.

5 **Look at the sentences. Can you think of a job for each one?**

1 I work in an office.

2 I wear a uniform.

3 I'm interested in art and music.

4 I like maths and science.

6 **Do you know the names of the jobs in the photos? Circle the words in the word snake.**

dentistpirateteacherastronautdoctorpoliceofficersingerpilotfirefighter

7 🔊 22 **Helen, Katy and Robert are talking about jobs. What do they want to do? Listen and tick (✓).**

1 Katy

2 Helen

3 Robert

8 **Complete the sentences with jobs.**

1 I've flown to a lot of different countries in my job. I'm a _____pilot_____ .

2 I've travelled up into space. I'm an _____ .

3 I've stopped a lot of houses from burning and helped a lot of people. I'm a _____ .

4 I've worked on TV and in the theatre. People like my music. I'm a _____ .

5 I've helped people and caught many bad people. I'm a _____ _____ .

1 Look at the places. Who works in each place?
Write the correct word on the lines.

1 _____farmer_____

2 _____

3 _____

farmer   waiter
ambulance driver   actor
business person

4 _____

5 _____

2 👁 George is talking about the job he likes best. Which job does he want to do most now?

These jobs are all good, but I want a job that's interesting and different every day. My dad wants me to be an engineer, **1** _____ I think my maths is really bad, so I don't want to do that job.

I'd like to be **2** _____ ambulance driver most. If you're an ambulance driver, you **3** _____ drive faster than the other cars, because you are helping people who are very ill. I think I have the right skills for this job. I'm very calm and I like helping people. My teacher says I can speak well and I'm friendly and kind **4** _____ people. I'm also good **5** _____ science. I've learned a lot about the human body. I don't know if I will do this because I'm too young to choose yet.

3 🚇23 ✏ Listen and write the words on the lines in task 2.

to   but   can   an   at

4 Complete the sentences with your ideas.

I'd like to be _____ because _____ .

I'm good at _____ .

_____ .

5 👁 **Look at the photo of William. What kind of hobbies do you think he has? Read the story. What is William's hobby? Why aren't his family happy about it?**

6 👁 **Read the story again. Write some words to complete the sentences about the story. You can use 1, 2, 3 or 4 words.**

William's business plan

William was playing a computer game. 'William!' called his mother from the kitchen. 'Can you come and help me?' But William didn't hear. 'What are you doing?' said his mother. 'I'm winning all the golden coins at the top of the mountain!' said William. His mother was not very happy. 'You're playing too many games,' she said. 'Don't play any more tonight.'

The next day the family were all in the garden … except one! 'William,' said his father, 'the picnic is ready. Come out and have some sandwiches.'

'OK,' said William, 'but can I come in ten minutes? I haven't finished my game!' His father was not very happy. 'You're playing on the computer too much. It isn't good for you.'

In the evening William did his homework. His eyes ached and he was very tired. He couldn't do his homework very well. The next day his teacher talked to him. 'I know you are very good at using computers,' she said, 'but you need to learn about lots of different things and you need to spend time with other people too. How will you find a good job when you are older if you only play games all alone?'

William went home. He sat down at his computer. His mother and father were both angry.

'William!' they said. 'Do something different!'

'I am doing something different!' said William. 'Look!'

Later that day his sister came home. 'Is William playing games again?' she asked.

'No,' said their mother. She was smiling. 'He's working!'

'I decided to use my skills in a better way!' said William. 'Look! I have my own website – William's Gaming World! I'm writing about the different games and how good they are. And I'm going to start a game club with my friends. When I'm older I want to be a journalist – so this is great practice. I'm even writing a business plan.'

'That's great!' said his sister. 'Shall we play a game now?'

William shook his head. 'No,' he said. 'I think we should go to the park. Working on the computer makes me feel tired. Let's do something different!'

Examples:

William didn't _____*listen to*_____ his mother.

His mother was angry because he was _____*playing too many*_____ games.

1 She told him to _____ playing.

2 The next day his family _____ picnic in the garden.

3 William wanted to _____ game before he went to the garden.

4 William did his homework badly because he felt very _____ .

5 William showed his sister his _____ .

6 She thought it was _____ .

7 William didn't want to _____ with her.

Review Unit 7

Skills: Writing and Speaking

1 How many places can you see in the word cloud? Draw circles.

Mark: ___ / 5

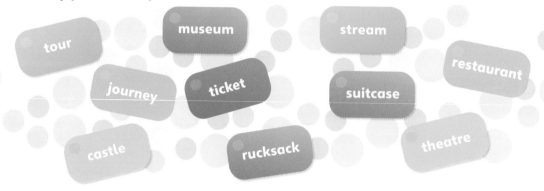

tour   museum   stream   restaurant

journey   ticket   suitcase

castle   rucksack   theatre

2 Which other words can you see about holidays?

_____

_____

3 Answer the questions. Use the places from task 1.

Mark: ___ / 5

1 This is a big building for lots of people and I can watch actors here. _____

2 This place has a lot of old things in it. I can learn about history here. _____

3 This is like a small river. _____

4 This is a big building and a king might have lived in it. _____

5 I can eat dinner here. It is where a waiter works. _____

Mark: ___ / 5

4 Choose three other words from the word cloud and write a clue for each one. Ask and answer with a friend.

5 Write the names under each photo.

Mark: ___ / 3

1 _____

2 _____

3 _____

4 _____

5 _____

6 _____

Mark: ___ / 6

Total: ___ / 24

Skills: Reading and Speaking

1 Write the names of the jobs under the photos.

COOL JOBS! WHAT DO YOU WANT TO BE?

There are a lot of interesting jobs in the world. Do you know what you want to do? Would you like to be a singer **1** _____ a police officer for example? They are interesting **2** _____ remember, a job that sounds fun might not be the best one for you. Firefighters have exciting jobs, **3** _____ if you don't like danger, you won't enjoy it. Instead, think about your skills **4** _____ you can find jobs that are interesting **5** _____ that you will be good at.

A _____

B _____

C _____

D _____

E _____

F _____

Mark: ___ / 6

2 Look at the words in the box. They are used to join sentences. Draw lines to the meanings.

1 gives two things to choose from

3 shows why something happens

so   but   and   or

2 shows two ideas that don't agree

4 adds a new idea

Mark: ___ / 4

3 Now read the text above and complete the sentences with the words from task 2.

Mark: ___ / 5

4 Talk to a friend. Say three sentences. Do you have the same ideas?

1 I'd like to be a _____ or a _____ because _____ .

2 I think _____ sounds interesting but I don't want to do it because _____ .

3 I think you're good at _____ , so you could be a _____ .

Mark: ___ / 3

Total: ___ ___ / 18

ANNA PAVLOVA

Have you ever eaten a pavlova? You should try it – it's a delicious dessert that's made of cooked eggs, sugar, cream and fruit. But most people don't know that the cook who invented it, named it after a real person. Anna Pavlova was a Russian ballet dancer. She started dance school when she was ten and worked very hard to become a brilliant dancer. She travelled all over the world, dancing in lots of different countries. Don't you think her beautiful, light, white dress looks like the pavlova?

Lionel Messi

Lots of people think that Lionel Messi is the best ever footballer because he was the youngest player to win four Ballons d'Or. The Ballon d'Or is a prize for the best footballer each year. Messi has scored the most goals for his home country, Argentina – 65 goals! He also scored the most goals ever in one year (2012) – he scored 91 goals in just 69 games of football! Messi lives in Spain and loves playing video games with his son.

Edward Jenner

Would you like to save people's lives? Some people think that the work of Edward Jenner has saved 530 million lives! This scientist is famous for helping to stop a dangerous illness called *smallpox*. He saw that people who worked with cows didn't catch smallpox and he used this information to learn more about the illness. Soon, he found a way to stop people getting smallpox at all. He was an amazing scientist!

---

1 👁 **When do you think they lived? Read, look and match the people to the dates. Then say why they are famous.**

> 1749–1823   1881–1931   1987–still living

2 ✏ **Read the texts again. Use the words in the box to write the questions for the answers.**

> What   ~~When~~   Who   Why   Where   What

1 When she was ten years old. _____ *When did Anna Pavlova start dance school?*

2 It's a dangerous illness. _____

3 He was an amazing scientist who wanted to help sick people. _____

4 Because he was the youngest player to win four Ballons d'Or. _____

5 Cooked eggs, sugar, cream and fruit. _____

6 Spain. _____

3 💬 **Ask and answer with a friend.**

1 What kind of food would you like to take your name? Why?

2 Would you prefer to be a famous dancer, a famous footballer or a famous scientist? Why?

3 What else would you like to be famous for? Why?

4 **Read the questions and match them to the answers A–F. Answer the questions for you.**

1 What's your favourite food? — `B` _____

2 Where would you like to go on holiday? — ☐ _____

3 What makes you laugh? — ☐ _____

4 What kind of clothes do you usually wear? — ☐ _____

5 Do you prefer music, reading or walking in the countryside? — ☐ _____

6 What is in your pockets right now? — ☐ _____

A Some sweets, my phone and a pencil.

B That's easy. Strawberry yoghurt.

C That's difficult, but I think I love playing the piano the most.

D Mm, let me think. My school uniform!

E To a beach where I can swim and sail.

F Mm, I don't know. Maybe it's my dog. He's very silly!

5 💬 **Ask and answer with a friend.**

What's your favourite food?

That's difficult. I think I like pasta salad the most.

TIP! When you need more time to think, try saying:

Mm, let me think.
Mm, I don't know. Maybe it's …
That's difficult but …

6 ✏️ **Now choose a famous person and think about him or her. Write his or her answers to the questions in task 4. They don't have to be true.**

1 _____

2 _____

3 _____

4 _____

5 _____

6 _____

7 💬 **Interview a friend. Which famous person do you think he or she is?**

1 🔊 24 **Listen and draw lines. There is one example.**

Sue   Paul   Amy

Asma   John   Sally   Peter

2 💬 **Which name didn't you use? Who do you think it is? What do you think they are famous for?**

> I think this person is called … .
> He/she might be famous for playing the guitar.

3 👁 Read about Serena Williams. Which facts do you think are the most important and the least important? Number the facts from 1 (most important) to 5 (least important).

Name: _Serena Williams_   Lived from: _1981_ to _still living._

Famous for: _being one of the best tennis players in the world._

Five facts

A She was 14 when she played in her first tennis competition.

E Her favourite animals are dogs and tigers.

1 D Serena Williams has won the most women's tennis competitions ever.

B She has also won four Olympic gold medals.

SERENA YOU'RE OUR INSPIRATION

C Serena's a fashion designer when she isn't playing tennis. She loves clothes.

4 Read and match the sentence halves.

1 Serena won her first big
2 Messi has lived in Spain
3 When Anna Pavlova wasn't dancing,
4 Messi has never

A won the World Cup.
B for most of his life.
C competition when she was 17.
D she was travelling and acting.

5 💬 Pairwork. Student A go to page 67. Student B go to page 68. Ask and answer questions.

10 Let's go to space!

I want to be an **1**_____ ,
And fly around the **2** _____ .
I want to take a **3** _____ to the stars.
I want to see all of the **4** _____ .
In just one afternoon,
And take photos of Jupiter and Mars.
I think I will be fine,
But how will I feel?
Alone in a **5** _____ ?
Looking down at planet **6** _____ far away?
How sad will I be,
When all that I can see
Is **7** _____ , on my space holiday?
I think I will be fine,
I still want to be a space-girl,
I just need to take a friend,
Travelling with a friend is always fun.
I think I will be fine,
With a favourite friend of mine,
When I'm flying past the hot, red **8** _____ .

1 🔊 **25** **Listen to the song and write the missing words. Them look and number the photos in the order you hear them.**

| sun   clouds   astronaut   spaceship   moon   rocket   Earth   stars   planets   aliens |

2 🔊 **25** **Listen again and answer the questions.**

1 What does the singer want to do?

2 What does she worry about?

3 What does she decide to do at the end of the song?

3 🔊 **25** **Sing the song.**

4 👁 ✏️ **Read the sentences with a friend. Write T (true) or F (false).**

1 The moon is the only thing astronauts have walked on in space. _____

2 Space begins 5 km above planet Earth. _____

3 There's no air in space, so astronauts take air with them from Earth. _____

4 A space station is a place where astronauts can live and work in space. _____

5 People invented rockets about 100 years ago. _____

6 The sun is a planet like Earth or Mars. _____

5 🔊 26 **Listen and check your answers. What other information did you hear? Can you write any of it in your notebook?**

6 ✏️ **Work with a friend to complete the table. Write a sentence about what you think will happen in 2025 or 2050.**

> What happened in 1942?

> In 1942, the first ... travelled into space.

> What will happen in 2025?

> In 2025 the first ... will ...

Date	What happened/What will happen?
1942	
1947	
1961	
1969	
1998	
2001	
2025	
2050	

7 ✏️ **Would you like to go on holiday to space? Why? / Why not? Write a sentence.**

I wouldn't like to go on holiday to space because it might be very cold and there aren't any people there.

I would like to go on holiday to space because ...

1 **Look at the picture and read the story. Write some words to complete the sentences on page 53 about the story. You can use 1, 2, 3 or 4 words.**

An amazing adventure

Last Saturday, Holly and Michael visited their cousin June. June is a scientist who studies space. When they arrived, June said,

'Let's have an adventure. Where shall we go?'

'The beach!' said Michael.

'How about a museum?' said Holly.

They were surprised when June said, 'Those places are boring. Let's go to the moon!'

June showed them her space rocket.

'I built this last year,' she said.

Holly and Michael felt excited, but a bit worried about travelling to the moon in it.

'Don't worry!' said June. 'It's very safe.'

They put on special clothes and helmets and they got into the rocket. June pushed 'Start' and they quickly flew off.

When the rocket landed, they jumped onto the moon.

'Wow!' said Holly. 'Space is beautiful! Look at all the stars and planets.'

'You can use the cameras in your helmets,' said June.

Holly and Michael took lots of photos. They were sad when June told them it was time to go home.

'We've just got here!' said Michael.

'Actually, we've been here for hours,' said June. 'And I'm hungry.'

They got into the rocket and flew back to Earth. They were tired that evening, but they were happy, too. They ate pizza and looked at their photos.

'What an amazing adventure!' said Holly. 'Thank you, June!'

Examples:

Holly and Michael's ___cousin___ is called June.

June is ___a scientist___ and she's interested in space.

Questions

1   Last Saturday, June wanted to take her cousins to _____ .

2   June made her _____ last year.

3   They put on _____ before they got in the rocket.

4   The rocket travelled _____ into the sky.

5   There were _____ in the helmets and they took photos.

6   June wanted to go home because she _____ .

7   They had _____ for dinner that evening.

2 How are they feeling? Read the text again in task 1 and <u>underline</u> seven *feeling* words. Draw an emoji for each word.

3 What's it *like*? Read the story again and circle five words for what things are *like* in the story.

4 🖊 Read the short story and complete the sentences with words from task 2 and 3.

MY TRIP TO SPACE

Last weekend, my mum said, 'Let's visit a new planet in space!' 'OK,' I said, but

I felt a bit **1** _____ .

We put on some **2** _____ clothes and got into our **3** _____

spaceship. I felt **4** _____ before we left. We travelled quickly through the sky and I was very

5 _____ when we landed.

The planet was **6** _____ and **7** _____ . There were some **8** _____

plants on it and we could see some **9** _____ planets in the sky near us. We played football

and had a picnic and then my mum felt **10** _____ . We got back into the rocket and flew

home. 'What a(n) **11** _____ adventure,' said my mum. 'Yes,' I said. I was very

12 _____ .

5 🖊 Imagine you have been on a trip to space. Write a short story about it. Use the questions to help you.

- When did you go?
- What did you wear?
- What did you do there?

- Who did you go with?
- How did you travel there?
- How did you feel?

Review Unit 9

Skills: Reading and Speaking

1 Read about Marta, John and Tessa's hobbies and write the correct words in the gaps.

> make   taking   went   going   visited   sell

MARTA

My favourite hobby is **1** _____ photographs. I often go to the forest or the beach and take photos of animals and birds. Sometimes I **2** _____ them to magazines or enter competitions. My friends think I'm a brilliant photographer, but I'm never happy with my photos. I think they could be better.

My parents have a restaurant and they taught me to cook when I was really young. Now I help them **3** _____ food in the kitchen at the weekends. Sometimes I also work as a waiter in the restaurant. People always think it's funny that a 12-year-old boy is their waiter! I'm also in a band and sometimes we play at my parents' restaurant. We're called the Skating Dolls. We're **4** _____ to be famous!

JOHN

TESSA

I've been playing tennis for eight years. My mum gave me my first racket when I was four! Then, when I was eight, I **5** _____ to a famous tennis camp in Spain. This really helped me to get better at tennis. I learned a lot and I won my first competition there. I practise every day and I've **6** _____ lots of interesting places to play tennis. I want to be the best in the world!

Mark: ___ / 6

2 Answer the questions.

1   How old was Tessa when she won her first competition? _____

2   Which three different ways does John help at the restaurant to make it successful?

_____

3   Who has travelled a lot? _____

4   Who is interested in the environment? _____

5   What important present did Tessa get when she was younger? _____

6   Does Marta think she is an amazing photographer? Why? / Why not?

_____

Mark: ___ / 6

3 Read the texts again and tell a friend.

1   Who do you think has the most interesting hobby? Why? / Why not?

2   Who do you think will be famous? Why? / Why not?

3   Would you like to be famous? Why? / Why not?

Mark: ___ / 3

Total: _____ / 15

Skills: Listening and Writing

1 🔊 27 **Listen to the story about Ben the astronaut and draw lines.**

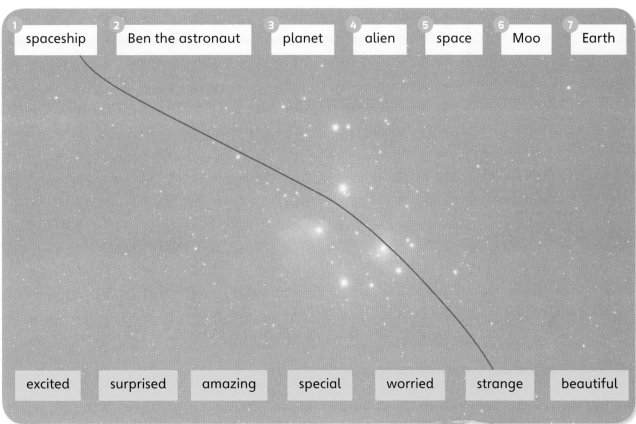

| 1 spaceship | 2 Ben the astronaut | 3 planet | 4 alien | 5 space | 6 Moo | 7 Earth |

| excited | surprised | amazing | special | worried | strange | beautiful |

Mark: ___ / 6

2 🔊 27 **Listen again and complete the sentences. You can use 1, 2 or 3 words.**

1 Ben the astronaut found _____ _____ in his garden.

2 The spaceship was orange with _____ _____ .

3 The planet had lots of _____ _____ and yellow grass on it.

4 Ben met an alien who had long _____ _____ .

5 Ben decided to _____ _____ back to Earth to find Moo.

6 Moo _____ in Ben's garden.

Mark: ___ / 6

3 **Why do you think Moo was worried? Write one sentence.**

_____

_____

_____

CHECKLIST

☐ I checked my spelling.

☐ My handwriting is clear.

☐ My answer makes sense.

Mark: ___ / 3

Total: ___ / 15

11 The Winter Olympics

1 💬 **Look at the picture. What can you see?**

2 **Draw lines from the words to the picture.** runner | stadium | ice | Olympic rings | torch

3 👁 **Read about the Olympic Games.**

The Olympic Games first started in Ancient Greece nearly 2,700 years ago. The games were held in the city of Olympia and a fire was burnt during the days that the Games happened. Now a **1** _____ still brings the Olympic **2** _____ to the Games and lights a fire. The symbol for the Olympics is the **3** _____ : these are five coloured circles. Each ring is there to show a different continent in the world and the rings are all joined together for the Games. At the Olympics, sports include running, high jump and swimming. The first Winter Olympics was in 1924. At the Winter Olympics people compete in sports on snow and **4** _____ . The main **5** _____ has an ice rink for these kinds of sports and has seats for over 35,000 thousand people.

4 **Write the words from task 2 on the lines.**

5 **Look at the numbers. Write questions. There is one example.**
1 How _many circles are there in the Olympic symbol_____ ? Five.
2 When _____ ? 2,700 years ago.
3 When _____ ? 1924.
4 How many _____ ? Over 35,000

6 💬 **Cover the questions and try to remember the information in task 5. Ask and answer with a friend.**

7 Put the letters in the correct order to make words. Then match them to the pictures.

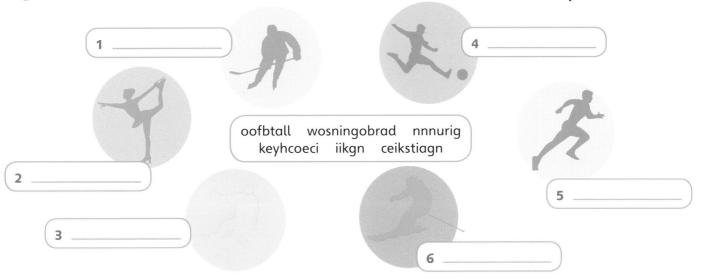

1 _____

4 _____

oofbtall wosningobrad nnnurig
keyhcoeci iikgn ceikstiagn

2 _____

5 _____

3 _____

6 _____

8 Read the first part of the TV guide. What happens at 9 am?

9.00 am	**The opening ceremony** Remember to join us on Channel Five tomorrow for the opening ceremony of the Olympic **1** Races / Games. The competition starts when the Olympic **2** torch / light arrives. It is carried **3** on / in to the stadium by a runner and used to light a fire. This will continue to **4** burn / fire until the end of the Winter Games. **5** See / Join us in the amazing new Olympic **6** field / stadium where there are enough seats for 35,000 people.

9 28 Circle the correct words. Then listen and check.

10 29 Read the rest of the TV guide. Write the red words on the red lines and the blue words on the blue lines. Then listen and check.

winner ski race gold fall over clap

2.00 pm	Our first **1** _____ of the Games begins! Watch the competitors **2** _____ down the beautiful mountains at high speed. Will any of them **3** _____ ? Who will be the fastest? Who will be the **4** _____ ?
4.00 pm	**5** _____ and cheer as the winner gets the **6** _____ medal!

11 Match the words.

1 on   A the sports stadium

2 for   B 2 pm

3 in   C the ice

4 at   D three weeks

5 since   E last year

12 Answer the questions with a friend.

1 Where do you do sports at or after school?

2 How long have you done your favourite sport?

3 When is your next sports lesson or game?

1 Look at the picture of the 'skeleton'. What do you think happens in this sport?

2  Alex does the skeleton at the Winter Olympic Games. Read Alex's diary and answer the questions.

1 How does Alex stop the sledge?

2 How fast does it go?

3 When did Alex start doing the skeleton?

4 Why is it important to keep your hands on the top?

3 Read the text again and write the missing words. Write one word on each line.

Alex's diary

Example: Today I ___am___ practising the skeleton. It is quite a dangerous sport, but I enjoy it. I need to be strong and healthy because it is hard work.

1 I lie down on a sledge. It _____ very small and I have to make it go left or right by moving my body. The sledge moves down a hill on the ice to the finish line.

2 If I want the sledge _____ stop I put my feet on the ice to slow it down. It can move very fast – over 125 kilometres per hour. I have

3 _____ a sportsman since I was 10 so I am not frightened. I have done lots of sports that are fast before – for example skiing.

4 The sledge has metal parts underneath _____ move over the ice quickly so it is important to keep your hands on top. I would like to go

5 faster _____ anyone else in the competition and win the gold medal!

TIP! When you have completed the gaps, make sure you re-read the text and check your answers.

4 Would you like to try the skeleton? Why? / Why not? Tell a friend.

5 Choose three or four sports from the Winter Olympics. Do a survey. Which is most popular?

6 💬 **Look at the pictures of Olympic mascots and read the description. Which do you like best? Why? Tell a friend.**

> A mascot is an animal or character used to advertise an event.
> Some people think mascots are lucky, so they are often used in sport.

7 👁 **Read Boyao's message to a friend. Answer the questions.**

Hello Eun!

Look at my photo of the White Tiger mascot! Isn't it great? I was visiting the sports stadium to watch ice skating. It was standing in the street and I stopped and took a photo. It looked amazing and it was very friendly. It's white and black and it has the Olympic rings on its chest. Its name is Sooho. This means 'protect' because it protects the Games and all the people there. I hope you like it!

See you soon,

Boyao ☺

1 Why did she like the mascot?
2 What does it look like?
3 Where did she take the photo?

8 **Work in a group. Can you draw a new Winter Olympics mascot? Think about colours and symbols.**

Dear _____

Look at my photo of _____ .
I was _____ and I stopped and
took a photo. She/he/it looked _____ .
_____
_____ . Its name is _____ because
_____ .

I hope you like it. See you soon!

9 ✏ **Now write a message to another group about your mascot. Say where you took the photo, what your mascot looks like and what it was like.**

12 Comics!

1 You see these shapes in comic strips and sometimes in cartoons. What do they show? Draw lines.

1   **2**   **3**

A Someone is thinking   **B** Wow! A surprise!   **C** Someone is saying something

2 🔊30 Look at the comic strip about Emma and Katy. Put the pictures into the correct order. Then listen and check.

3 Read the story below. Can you complete it? Write the words on the lines.

> ~~bedroom~~   tennis   bored   idea   playing   wearing

Emma was in her **1** _bedroom_ with her friend Katy. 'What's wrong?' asked Katy. I'm **2** _____ !' said Emma. Katy thought carefully. 'How about a game of **3** _____ ?' she said. 'Or we could read a magazine?' But Emma didn't want to. 'I don't like **4** _____ tennis,' she said. 'And I don't like reading magazines. I only like reading comics or playing computer games. And I like fish.' Katy and Emma thought hard. 'Ah!' they said. 'I know!' They both had a good **5** _____ .

Emma opened her dressing up box. Ten minutes later she was ready. 'Watch out!' she said. 'Here comes 'Superfish' to save the day!' Emma was **6** _____ her Superfish clothes. 'You look great!' said Katy. 'Let me take a picture of Superfish for your blog!' They weren't bored any more.

4 💬 Work with a friend. Tell the story again using the pictures.

5 Look at the picture. Which country do you think this comic book is from?

6 🔊 31 Listen to Emma talking about comics and computer games. Answer the questions.

1 When was the first comic strip made?

2 Which country sells the most comic books?

3 Which superheroes are in computer games too?

7 🔊 31 Listen again. Which is Emma's favourite character from a computer game? Tick (✓) the correct picture.

8 🖊 Work with a friend. Think of your own superhero for a comic or computer game. Complete the table with information about your superhero.

Name of the character:	
What he/she looks like:	
What he/she wears:	
Super skill:	

9 💬 Talk to another friend. Ask questions about their character and tell them about your character.

> What's the name of your character?

> He's called Metal Man!

> What is his super skill?

> He's big and strong. He can lift cars!

1 🔊 32 👁 **Look at the pictures. Where did Emma and Katy go? Do you think they enjoyed it? Now read, listen and check.**

Emma and Katy were bored. They tried watching TV, but there weren't any interesting programmes. They tried playing volleyball, but it was too hot. They even tried reading Emma's old 'Superfish' comics, but she had read them all before.

They decided to go to the aquarium. The aquarium was a big building near the river and it was full of interesting sea creatures. There were a lot of different fish and animals there. 'I'm glad we came!' said Emma. 'It's a great idea!'

Emma liked the dolphins and the spotted fish. Katy liked the sharks. They both wanted to see the octopus, but it was behind some plants and they couldn't.

'Let's go to the café,' said Emma. 'I'm thirsty'. They bought some lemonade and some pizza and they sat down at a table. The café was very nice because there were windows all along the wall and they could see into the tanks where the fish lived. They could watch the fish while they were eating and drinking.

'I had a great time,' said Katy, 'But it's a shame we didn't see the octopus.' Emma was smiling. 'Look!' she said to Katy. She was pointing at the window. Katy turned around. The octopus was in the window very close up. It was next to them. 'Wow!' said Emma and Katy. 'We have the best view!'

2 🔊 32 👁 **Read and listen to the story again. Answer the questions.**

1 Why did they go to the aquarium?

2 What did they both want to see?

3 Why was the café a good place to go?

3 👁 **Read the story again and write one word on each line.**

1 Emma and Katy were bored so they went to the _____ to see the fish.

2 Emma liked the dolphins and Katy liked the sharks but they both wanted to see the _____ .

3 They couldn't see it because it was behind some _____ .

4 They decided to go to the café and get some food and _____ .

5 While they were in the café, they saw the octopus through the _____ .

6 They were both very _____ .

4 💬 **Work with a friend. Tell the story again using the pictures.**

5 ✏️ **Look at the three pictures. Write about this story. Write 20 or more words.**

6 💬 **Work with a friend. Tell your story.**

CHECKLIST

☐ I looked at the pictures first to understand the story.

☐ I wrote one or two sentences about each picture.

☐ I wrote between 20 and 30 words.

Review Unit 11

Skills: Writing and Speaking

1 Which hobby do Sam, Jo and Pat have? Number the pictures 1, 2, 3.

> reading magazines   watching cartoons   playing volleyball

A

B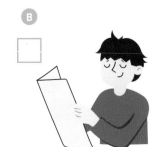

C

1 loves reading and learning.

Sam likes _____

2 enjoys this when they are on TV.

Jo likes _____

3 often goes outside to do some sport.

Pat likes _____

Mark: ___ / 6

2 Which words can go together? Copy the 3 shapes and words into your notebook and write the words around the correct shape.

> ~~football~~ ice hockey   interesting   competition   volleyball   amazing   cartoon   race   fun

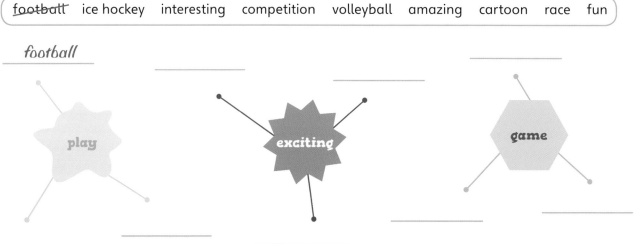

football

play   *exciting*   *game*

Mark: ___ / 8

3 Can you add two more words to each group? Work in pairs. What kind of word did you add to each group – a verb, noun or adjective?

Mark: ___ / 6

4 Match the beginning and ends of the sentences to make questions. Then ask and answer with a partner.

1 Have you ever   A computer game?

2 Which competition is more   B exciting, football or ice skating?

3 What is your favourite cartoon or   C won a race?

Mark: ___ / 6

Total: ___ ___ / 26

Skills: Reading and Speaking

1 **Read about 'Winter Adventure Land' and write words on the lines.**

Welcome to Winter Adventure Land! Come along for a fun weekend in the

0 _snow_ ❄️ . You can stay in an amazing **1** _____ 🏨 and eat some

good food. You can try **2** _____ ⛷️ or you might prefer **3** _____ 🏂 .

You could even make a **4** _____ ⛄ . In the evening, you can watch a

5 _____ 📺 on TV or read a **6** _____ 📖 . If you prefer, you can play

7 _____ ♟️ by the **8** _____ 🔥 . You'll have a great time, so come soon!

Mark: ___ / 8

2 **Work with a friend. What kind of 'Adventure Land' would you like?**
Make notes in the table.

Name of place:
Place to stay:
Things to do in the day:
Things to do in the evening:

3 **Find a new friend. Ask and answer.**

Mark: ___ / 4

What's the name of your place?

It's called Game Land.

Oh great! It sounds fun. Do you have a hotel?

No, but you can stay in a game tent. It has comics in it and some computer games …

Mark: ___ / 5

4 **How many new words do you remember? Choose three words from unit 11 and 12.**
Write down an example for each one. Test a friend. Can they guess your word?

Mark: ___ / 3

Total: ___ / 20

Pairwork

Unit 4 page 22

Student B

Look at the information about two animals.

Ask and answer questions and complete the information.

	Octopus	Beetles
Like eating	Small sea creatures	Leaves, fruit, wood
Where	In the ocean	Dark places – forests, gardens
Dangerous for people?	Some are dangerous	Not usually

Like eating		
Where		
Dangerous for people?		

Unit 9 page 47

Student A

Look at the information about famous people. You have information about Lionel Messi but you don't know anything about Serena Williams. Ask and answer questions with Student B.

Lionel fun facts

Surname	Messi
Nationality	Argentinian
Colour / like	Red
Hobbies	Video games and music
Like eating	Escalope Milanese and salad

Serena fun facts

Surname	?
Nationality	?
Colour / like	?
Hobbies	?
Like eating	?

Pairwork

Unit 9 page 47

Student B
Look at the information about famous people. You have information about
Serena Williams but you don't know anything about Lionel. Ask and answer
questions with Student A.

Serena fun facts

Surname	Williams
Nationality	American
Colour / like	Gold
Hobbies	Reading and watching movies
Like eating	Fried chicken and sushi

Messi fun facts

Surname	?
Nationality	?
Colour / like	?
Hobbies	?
Like eating	?

Unit 10 page 50

I want to be an astronaut,
And fly around the moon.
I want to take a rocket to the stars.
I want to see all of the planets
In just one afternoon,
And take photos of Jupiter and Mars.
I think I will be fine
But how will I feel?
Alone in a spaceship?
Looking down at planet earth far away?
How sad will I be,
When all that I can see
Is stars on my space holiday?
I think I will be fine
I still want to be a space-girl,
I just need to take a friend,
Travelling with a friend is always fun.
I think I will be fine
With a favourite friend of mine,
When I'm flying past the hot, red sun.

Unit 1

Tag questions

✓ ✗ It looks wonderful, **doesn't it?**	Yes, it does.
✗ ✓ It doesn't look fun, **does it?**	No, it looks scary.
✓ ✗ That's Holly's bike, **isn't it?**	Yes, I think it is.
✗ ✓ That isn't Holly's bike, **is it?**	No, it's Emma's.

You aren't doing your homework, **are you?**
We cooked the noodles, **didn't we?**
They were playing golf, **weren't they?**
She hasn't visited London, **has she?**

1 Match the questions to the tags.

1 Oliver went home early,   A don't they?
2 Maria and Marco like
   pancakes,   B do they?
3 Betty's at the theatre,   C isn't she?
4 Nick and Elif don't study
   geography,   D is she?
5 Richard didn't join the club,   E didn't he?
6 Helen isn't in the library,   F did he?

2 Write tags for the questions.

1 George and Frank don't have sunglasses,

   _____ ?

2 Your sister Sarah's 13 now,

   _____ ?

3 You've entered the competition,

   _____ ?

4 George and Katy weren't in the playground,

   _____ ?

5 Sophia was watching TV,

   _____ ?

6 It isn't raining,

   _____ ?

Unit 2

Adverbs of frequency: *usually, much*

It's usually small.
Usually, it's small.
It's small **usually**.

Frank usually stays at home. He **doesn't** go out **much**.

1 Match the sentences.

1 Helen's busy all week.
2 She's good at snowboarding.
3 Her cat's always hungry.
4 Her house is far away from school.
5 She lives in a hot country.

A She feeds her three times every day.
B She usually gets up late at the weekend.
C It doesn't snow much.
D Usually, she catches a bus.
E She doesn't fall over much.

2 Correct the words or word order.

1 Betty's baby brother has grown ~~much~~.

   _____ .

2 Sarah ~~brushes her usually~~ teeth before
   breakfast.

   _____ .

3 Richard and Robert don't ~~much~~ go to the
   park.

   _____ .

4 William ~~goes usually~~ to the playground after
   school.

   _____ .

5 Katy ~~much~~ goes swimming.

   _____ .

Grammar fun!

Unit 3

What time …?

> **What time** shall we meet?
> **What time** is it?
> **What time** is lunch?
> **What time** does the football match start?
> **What time** do Harry and Charlie get up?
> **What time** did you get up today?

1 **Put the questions in the correct order.**

1 is / what / art / time / club?

_____

2 what / we / time / dinner? / shall / have

_____

3 parents / time / come home? / do / your / what

_____

4 wake up? / time / you / what / did

_____

5 time / start? / what / does / school

_____

2 **Choose the correct word.**

1 What time **is** / **does** the show?

2 What time **do** / **are** Mattia and Katy go swimming?

3 What time **did** / **was** the test yesterday?

4 What time **did** / **was** your friends arrive?

5 What time **does** / **is** the train leave?

Unit 4

'Where is it / Where's it from?'

> This is **where polar bears live**.
> I've forgotten **where I put my phone**.

1 **Look and complete the sentences. Use the words in the box.**

> ~~birds~~   pandas   penguins   rabbits
> dolphins   camels

1

This is _where birds live_____ .

2

This is _____ .

3

This is _____ .

4

This is _____ .

5
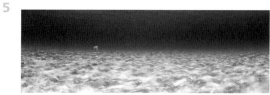
This is _____ .

6

This is _____ .

Unit 5

Verbs: *be going to*

✓	✗
I'm **going to** be hungry. He/She/It**'s going to** be hungry. You/We/They**'re going to** be hungry.	I'm **not going to** be hungry. He/She/It **isn't going to** be hungry. You/We/They **aren't going to** be hungry.

- **Is** it **going to** rain?
- Yes, it **is**. / No, it **isn't**.

1 Look and complete the sentences with *going to* and an expression from the box.

finish first   be late   watch a film   rain

1

He _____ .

2

It _____ .

3

They _____ .

2 Complete the sentences. Use *be going to* and the words in brackets.

1 George wants a new comic book.
He _____ . (ask his mum)

2 Betty and Helen have forgotten their scissors.
They _____

_____ .
(borrow Harry's)

3 Be careful! Your bag _____

_____ .(break)

Unit 6

Adverbs: *away*

The eagle saw us and flew **away**.
Go **away**!
David hates spiders, so he looked **away**.
Our teacher isn't at school. She's **away** today.

How far **away** is the theatre?
I live five minutes **away** from school.

1 Match the sentences to the photos.

1 It's flying away.   A

2 They're running away.   B

3 She's looking away.   C

4 They're going away.   D

5 She's taking the food away.   E

2 Put the sentences in the correct order.

1 far / house? / is / away / your / how
_____

2 away / school. / lives / far / Franco / his / from
_____

3 so / was / it / I / away. / scary / looked
_____

4 away / me. / cycled / from / David
_____

5 moved / tree. / panda / the / away / the / from
_____

Unit 7

Adverbs: *yet, already, ever, just*

Have you **ever** been to a castle?
No, I haven't been to a castle **yet**. I hope we'll have time to go.

Would you like to go to the castle?
I've **already** been to the castle. I went there last summer.
I've **just** been to the castle. I went there this morning. But I've **never** been to the castle museum!

1 Complete the sentences with *yet*, *already* or *just*.

1

The plane's _____ landed.

2

They haven't finished _____ .

3

She's _____ scored a goal.

4

They haven't paid _____ .

5

He _____ knows the answer.

2 Add the word in brackets to the sentences.

1 I haven't bought my sister's birthday present. (yet)

_____

2 Have you played chess? (ever)

_____

3 The rain's stopped. (just)

_____

4 David's finished the snowman. (already)

_____

Unit 8

Verbs: *shall* for suggestions

What **shall** we **do**?
Shall we **play** a game?
Shall I **call** you later?

1 Match the sentences with the suggestions.

1 I'm afraid of the dark.
2 This question's difficult.
3 It's warm and sunny.
4 This film's boring.
5 What shall we do at the zoo?

A Shall I ask the teacher?
B Shall we listen to some music instead?
C Shall I turn on the light?
D Shall we find the lions?
E Shall we have a picnic in the park?

2 Put the sentences in the correct order.

1 forest? / the / we / shall / explore

_____

2 we / puzzle? / shall / a / do

_____

3 play / we / board game? / a / shall

_____

4 a / shall / snowman? / build / we

_____

5 shall / what / do / school? / we / after

_____

Unit 9

○ *Make somebody/something + adjective*

The smell **made me hungry**.
Running **makes you thirsty**.
What **makes you laugh**?

1 Match the sentence halves.

1 Swimming   A makes you excited.

2 Going to bed late B makes you tired.

3 Practising   C makes you worried.

4 Having fun   D makes you wet.

5 Having a problem E makes you good at tennis.

2 Complete the sentences. Use the words in brackets.

1 Katy loves music. It

_____ . (make / her / happy)

2 The party was great. The games

_____ . (make / it / exciting)

3 I loved the pasta! Harry's sauce

_____ . (make / it / delicious)

4 That film

_____ . (make / the actor / famous)

5 - What

_____ ? (make / you / late)

- The bus didn't come, so I had to walk.

Unit 10

○ Adverbs: *actually*

- Have you just arrived?
- **Actually**, we've been here for hours. / We've **actually** been here for hours. / We've been here for hours, **actually**.

- Do you like football?
- Yes. **Actually**, I like lots of sports. / I **actually** like lots of sports. / I like lots of sports, **actually**.

1 Complete the conversations. Use *actually* and an expression from the box.

I dropped it I've been to lots I haven't started
I prefer puzzles the shop was closed
it's sunny now I went to the beach
I'd love an ice cream

1 - Would you like some food?

  - _____ .

2 - Have you finished the homework yet?

  - _____ .

3 - Did you do anything nice at the weekend?

  - _____ .

4 - Is it going to rain?

  - _____ .

5 - Did you catch the ball?

  - _____ .

6 - Do you like board games?

  - _____ .

7 - Did you buy some sweets?

  - _____ .

8 - Have you ever been to a castle?

  - _____ .

Grammar fun!

Unit 11

See you soon/later/tomorrow, etc.

See you soon, Eun!
See you later, George!
See you tomorrow, David!
See you on Friday!
See you at the weekend!
See you next week/month/year!

1 Make sentences. Use the words in the correct order.

1 _____ !
(later / see / you)

2 _____ !
(you / soon / see)

3 _____ !
(month / see / next / you)

4 _____ !
(tomorrow / you / see)

5 _____ !
(next / you / see / week)

2 Look at the calendar below. What will you say to the people? Complete the sentences.

1 *See you later* _____ , Oliver!
2 _____ , Katy!
3 _____ , Fatima!
4 _____ , José!
5 _____ , William!

Unit 12

Adverbs: *before*

She **had read** them all **before**.
Have you been here **before**?
Frank hasn't been to the beach **before**.
I've seen her **before**.

1 Complete the sentences. Use an expression from the box and *before*.

tried   been here   seen this film   met
heard it   played tennis

1 Sarah hasn't _____ . She doesn't know where the bathroom is.

2 Holly doesn't know Robert. They haven't _____ .

3 William knows that song. He's _____ .

4 Helen hasn't _____ . She's not very good yet.

5 George can't skate. He's _____ , but he kept falling over.

6 Betty and David are bored. They've _____ .

Monday 14th	Tuesday 15th	Wednesday 16th	Thursday 17th	Friday 18th	Saturday 19th	Sunday 20th
✕	✕	Meet Oliver	Katy	Meet Fatima		Meet José

Monday 21st	Tuesday 22nd	Wednesday 23rd	Thursday 24th	Friday 25th	Saturday 26th	Sunday 27th
			Meet William			

Unit 1+10

○ Tag questions & Adverbs: *actually*

1 Ask and answer the questions with a friend. Use tag questions in your questions. Use *actually* in your answers.

> You like football, don't you?

> Actually, I don't like football.

You like football, You go out on Saturdays,	don't you?
You aren't 16, You aren't tired,	are you?
You've been to the circus, You've seen a lion,	haven't you?
You haven't seen my phone, You haven't joined the club,	have you?

Unit 7

○ Adverbs: *yet, already, ever, just*

2 Ask and answer questions with a friend. Use *Would you like to ...* and the expressions in the box in your questions. Use *yet* or *already* in your answers.

> go to the castle   go shopping   have lunch
> watch the film   cook the noodles
> play the board game   go roller skating in the park

> Would you like to go to the castle?

> No. I've already been to the castle. /
> Yes. I haven't been to the castle yet.

Unit 3

Student A

○ *What time ...?*

5 Look at Katy's diary for last Saturday. Ask Student B what time Katy did the things in the box. Fill in the diary.

> play tennis   go to the cinema   go to bed
> have dinner

SATURDAY

8 am	get up
10 am	
12 pm	meet Holly
2 pm	
4 pm	go roller skating
6 pm	
8 pm	do some homework
10 pm	

> What time did Katy play tennis?

> She played tennis at ...

Grammar fun pairwork!

Unit 8

○ Verbs: *shall* for suggestions

3 **Decide with a friend what to do. Make suggestions with *shall*.**

It's cold outside.
What shall we do?

Shall we play a
board game.

OK, good idea!

1 It's cold outside.

2 I'm hungry.

3 Our bike's broken.

4 It's a lovely day.

5 School's finished.

Unit 9

○ *Make somebody/something + adjective*

4 **Ask and answer questions with a friend. Use *What makes you ...* and the words in the box in your questions.**

> happy sad hungry thirsty excited
> bored worried

What makes you happy?

Skipping makes me happy. And you?
What makes you happy?

Unit 3

Student B

○ *What time ...?*

5 **Look at Katy's diary for last Saturday. Ask a friend what time Katy did the things in the box. Fill in the diary.**

> go roller skating   meet Holly   get up
> do some homework

SATURDAY

8 am	
10 am	go to the cinema
12 pm	
2 pm	play tennis
4 pm	
6 pm	have dinner
8 pm	
10 pm	go to bed

What time did Katy
go roller skating?

She went roller skating
at ...

Listening Checklist

Circle , if your answer is Yes!

I can read and recognise English names when I hear them.

I listened to children talking about sports teams and filled in the information in task 1 on page 8.

I can write down names correctly when I hear them spelt out.

I listened to someone talking about a school club and filled in all the information in task 6 on page 17.

I can choose the correct picture when I hear it talked about.

I chose the correct place for each photo in task 3 on page 32.

I can understand all the colour words when I hear them.

I listened to Sarah talking about her holiday and chose the correct pictures of the things she hasn't done yet in task 7 on page 37.

I can draw things in the right place in a picture when I hear it described.

I answered questions about a song I heard about a girl who wants to be an astronaut in task 2 on page 50.

How many magic squirrels did you get?

Reading & Writing Checklist

Check your progress, colour the stars!

OK · Great

I can read a definition of a word and match it to the right word.

I know more than ten words about school.

I can read and understand sentences and put them in the right gaps in a dialogue.

I like reading stories in English.

I fill in the missing words in a text when I have the words to choose from.

I know more than ten words about animals.

I am good at matching expressions that go together in dialogues.

I can write a good ending to a story I have read.

I am good at grammar.

Reading & Writing Checklist

Circle 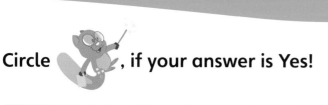, if your answer is Yes!

I wrote a description of a fun team with my friends in task 7 on page 7.

I matched the everyday objects words to their definitions in task 4 on page 11.

I matched the questions to the correct answers in task 5 on page 19.

I read and understood the text about food chains and chose the correct words and title in tasks 3 and 4 on page 23.

I chose the right words to fill in the gaps in the text about sugar in task 7 on page 27.

I wrote about my ideas for a picnic in task 1 on page 34.

I matched all the task 2 words to the correct photos in task 5 on page 37.

I read the story about Holly's holiday and put the photos in the correct order in tasks 2 and 3 on page 38.

I wrote the questions in the past tense to the answers about the famous people in task 2 on page 46.

I wrote an interesting message describing my sports mascot in task 9 on page 59.

How many magic squirrels did you get?

Speaking Checklist

Check your progress, colour the stars!

I can say how pictures are different by describing them carefully.

I found six differences in the pictures of a kitchen and told my friend about them in task 2 on page 11.

I can ask yes/no and wh- questions.

I talked with my friend about what the animals in the pictures might be and what they might eat in task 2 on page 22.

I can tell a story about pictures I see.

I told a story about the pictures in the jungle using lots of words from the box in task 7 on page 31.

I can answer questions about myself now, in the past and the future.

I talked with my friend about jobs we would like in task 4 on page 45.

I am very happy to speak in English.

I did a survey about winter sports and asked lots of my classmates about their favourites in task 5 on page 58.

Word list

Unit 1

chess *n* _____

competition *n* _____

delicious *adj* _____

environment *n* _____

fast *adv* _____

flag *n* _____

gym *n* _____

hate *v* _____

information *n* _____

interested *adj* _____

invent *v* _____

join (a club) *v* _____

meal *n* _____

meet *v* _____

million *n* _____

month *n* _____

prize *n* _____

puzzle *n* _____

race *v* _____

remember *v* _____

student *n* _____

summer *n* _____

team *n* _____

thousand *n* _____

Unit 2

butter *n* _____

comb *n* _____

cushion *n* _____

diary *n* _____

envelope *n* _____

fridge *n* _____

gate *n* _____

key *n* _____

king *n* _____

letter (as in mail) *n* _____

metal *adj+n* _____

newspaper *n* _____

oven *n* _____

plastic *n* _____

post *v* _____

queen *n* _____

shampoo *n* _____

shelf *n* _____

soap *n* _____

soft *adj* _____

speak *v* _____

stamp *n* _____

stone *n* _____

swing *n* _____

telephone *n* _____

toothbrush *n* _____

wood *n* _____

Unit 3

adventure *n* _____

astronaut *n* _____

biscuit *n* _____

business *n* _____

club *n* _____

design *n+v* _____

drum *n* _____

excited *adj* _____

geography *n* _____

hear *v* _____

horrible *adj* _____

meeting *n* _____

money *n* _____

noisy *adj* _____

rocket *n* _____

space *n* _____

Unit 4

beetle *n* _____

butterfly *n* _____

camel *n* _____

desert *n* _____

eagle *n* _____

insect *n* _____

nest *n* _____

octopus *n* _____

pond *n* _____

swan *n* _____

tortoise *n* _____

wing *n* _____

Unit 5

cookie (UK biscuit) *n* _____

forget *v* _____

group *n* _____

invitation *n* _____

jam *n* _____

olives *n* _____

pizza *n* _____

pyramid *n* _____

sugar *n* _____

tidy *adj* _____

umbrella *n* _____

yoghurt *n* _____

Unit 6

costume *n* _____

dinosaur *n* _____

enormous *adj* _____

follow *v* _____

frightening *adj* _____

fur *n* _____

job *n* _____

kilometre *n* _____

large *adj* _____

magazine *n* _____

spot *n* _____

Unit 7

airport *n* _____

bridge *n* _____

castle *n* _____

factory *n* _____

fire station *n* _____

hotel *n* _____

journey *n* _____

language *n* _____

museum *n* _____

ocean *n* _____

platform *n* _____

police station *n* _____

popular *adj* _____

restaurant *n* _____

skyscraper *n* _____

snowboarding *n* _____

south *n* _____

stream *n* _____

taxi *n* _____

tent *n* _____

university *n* _____

visit *v* _____

worried *adj* _____

Unit 8

actor *n* _____

ambulance *n* _____

engineer *n* _____

fire *n* _____

firefighter *n* _____

journalist *n* _____

mechanic *n* _____

minute *n* _____

office *n* _____

pilot *n* _____

planet *n* _____

science *n* _____

singer *n* _____

spend *v* _____

tonight *n* _____

uniform *n* _____

waiter *n* _____

Unit 9

date *n* _____

designer *n* _____

gold *adj* _____

pocket *n* _____

save *v* _____

strawberry *n* _____

Unit 10

arrive *v* _____

Earth *n* _____

hour *n* _____

land *v* _____

missing *adj* _____

push *v* _____

spaceship *n* _____

study *v* _____

thank *v* _____

Unit 11

burn *v* _____

fast *adj* _____

high *adj* _____

hill *n* _____

lie down *v* _____

race *n+v* _____

ring *n* _____

ski *n+v* _____

sledge *n+v* _____

stadium *n* _____

torch *n* _____

winner *n* _____

Unit 12

bored *adj* _____

cartoon *n* _____

programme *n* _____

sell *v* _____

spotted *adj* _____

surprise *n* _____

view *n* _____

volleyball *n* _____

In your book ...

Jo

Likes: homework, surprises

Dislikes: cats, milk

Kira

Likes: milk, stories

Dislikes: mice, watching TV

Himmy

Likes: maths, science

Dislikes: sports, rain

Jones

Likes: flying very high, fruit

Dislikes: swimming in the sea, vegetables

Clunk

Likes: computers, noodles

Dislikes: the sea, football

Sky

Likes: ice cream, purple

Dislikes: crocodiles

... from kids around the world

Lena, 11

Sezai, 12

Verity, 15

Mosés, 11

Jim Jung, 11

Leonor, 11

Hunter

Likes: apples, pizza

Dislikes: spiders, snails

Likes: pizza, apple juice, playing ball

Dislikes: ice cream, burgers, mice, cats

Likes: science, music, interesting animals, playing basketball

Dislikes: disorder, meat, destruction, black

Sage

Think Big Giraffe

Likes: plants

Dislikes: meat, lions

Likes: reading, eating, joking, art

Dislikes: pickles, flies, the dark, cockroaches

Anna, 10

Mariya, 8

Mario, 11

Adriana, 7

Edith, 11

Author acknowledgements

Bridget Kelly would like to thank Ann-Marie, Lynn and Anne - she really enjoyed working with them all. And thanks to Colin and little Aedan as always.

Stephanie Dymond-Bayir is grateful to the wonderful team of editorial staff and writers at CUP, Matthew, Ata and her mum.

Publisher acknowledgements

The authors and publishers are grateful to the following for reviewing the material during the writing process:

Selin Agullo: Turkey; Lucie Cotterill: Italy; Roisin O'Farrell: Spain; Georges Erhard: Vietnam; Ekaterina Degtyar: Russia; Gustavo Baron Sanchez: Mexico

The authors and publishers acknowledge the following sources of copyright material and are grateful for the permissions granted. While every effort has been made, it has not always been possible to identify the sources of all the material used, or to trace all copyright holders. If any omissions are brought to our notice, we will be happy to include the appropriate acknowledgements on reprinting and in the next update to the digital edition, as applicable.

Key: GR = Grammar; U = Unit.

Photography

The following photographs are sourced from Getty Images.

GR: Steve Satushek/Photodisc; 35007/E+; SinghaphanAllB/Moment; GYRO PHOTOGRAPHY; Jeff Rotman/Photolibrary/Getty Images Plus; whitemay/iStock/Getty Images Plus; Bigshots/DigitalVision; Abstract Aerial Art/DigitalVision; andresr/E+; FatCamera/E+; IMAGEMORE Co, Ltd.; John Lund/DigitalVision; Peter Mason/Cultura; Peter Muller/Cultura; Loop Images/Universal Images Group; Klaus Vedfelt/DigitalVision; John Giustina/The Image Bank/Getty Images Plus; Hill Street Studios/DigitalVision; Allen Donikowski/Moment/Getty Images Plus; Ada Summer/Corbis/VCG; energyy/E+; mikroman6/Moment; **U1:** ssj414/E+; Caiaimage/Robert Daly; Hero Images; David Leahy/DigitalVision; Rick Gomez; Aditya Sethia/EyeEm; SolStock/E+; **U2:** Dorling Kindersley/Getty Images Plus; photooiasson/iStock/Getty Images Plus; DEA/G. DAGLI ORTI; Image Source/DigitalVision; Pierre-Yves Babelon/Moment; Simon Eldon/ArcaidImages; **U3:** carrollphoto/E+; Hero Images; Henn Photography/Cultura; Fabrice LEROUGE/ONOKY; Aslan Alphan/iStock/Getty Images Plus; chris-mueller/iStock Editorial/Getty Images Plus; altrendo images/Stockbyte; LightFieldStudios/iStock/Getty Images Plus; Design Pics; Thomas Bullock/iStock/Getty Images Plus; JLBarranco/iStock/Getty Images Plus; Gustavo Huenchupán/EyeEm; Jose Luis Pelaez Inc/DigitalVision; Santiago Bañón/Moment; martinedoucet/E+; **U4:** Joel Sartore, National Geographic Photo Ark; Bryan Watson/EyeEm; angiii/iStock/Getty Images Plus; Pixelchrome Inc/DigitalVision; abadonian/iStock/Getty Images Plus; ByoungJoo/iStock/Getty Images Plus; Design Pics Inc/First Light/Getty Images Plus; Manuel Rodriguez/EyeEm; Kathy Kay/Moment; Joel Sartore, National Geographic Photo Ark/National Geographic Image Collection; Jonathan Knowles/Stone/Getty Images Plus; MarkGillow/E+; shikheigoh/RooM; Sandra Standbridge/Moment; ALBERTO GHIZZI PANIZZA/SCIENCE PHOTO LIBRARY/Science Photo Library; Kory Rogers/EyeEm; SL Liang/Moment; Peter Jenkins/EyeEm; **U5:** Westend61; STEEX/E+; pidjoe/E+; pechevoy/iStock/Getty Images Plus; EasyBuy4u/iStock/Getty Images Plus; MarkGillow/E+; Creativ Studio Heinemann; Burcu Atalay Tankut/Moment; PeskyMonkey/iStock/Getty Images Plus; Foodcollection RF; Foodcollection; Johner Images; Image Source; deepblue4you/E+; **U6:** Firefly Productions/Corbis/Getty Images Plus; Vicki Jauron, Babylon and Beyond Photography/Moment; kuritafsheen/RooM; Sciepro/Science Photo Library; cunfek/E+; Sumiko Scott/Moment Open; John Cancalosi/Photolibrary/Getty Images Plus; Edwin Remsberg/The Image Bank/Getty Images Plus; AFP; James Hager/robertharding/Getty Images Plus; Jacek Kadaj/Moment; Valter Jacinto/Moment; D. Sharon Pruitt Pink Sherbet Photography/Moment; Jamie Marshall - Tribaleye Images/The Image Bank/Getty Images Plus; Carlos G. Lopez/Moment; Jacobs Stock Photography Ltd/DigitalVision; David

Clapp/Oxford Scientific/Getty Images Plus; Martyn Ferry/Moment; SammyVision/Moment; Nacivet/Taxi/Getty Images Plus; View Pictures/Universal Images Group; John Guidi/robertharding/Getty Images Plus; **U7:** VichienPetchmai/iStock/Getty Images Plus; Pablo Cersosimo/robertharding; Arand/iStock/Getty Images Plus; yongyuan/iStock Unreleased; travelgame/Lonely Planet Images/Getty Images Plus; Panya Kuanun/EyeEm; leungchopan/iStock/Getty Images Plus; mammuth/iStock/Getty Images Plus; panso/iStock/Getty Images Plus; Steffen Schnur/Moment; KenWiedemann/iStock Unreleased; Feifei Cui-Paoluzzo/Moment; mustafagull/iStock/Getty Images Plus; Ruben Earth/Moment; Jan Starcke/EyeEm; d3sign/Moment; Wu Zhi Shen Mng/EyeEm; monkeybusinessimage/iStock/Getty Images Plus; Adie Bush/Cultura; Ariel Skelley/DigitalVision; Jose Manuel Espinola Aguayo/EyeEm; SerrNovik/iStock/Getty Images Plus; Ababsolutum/E+; Nicole Lienemann/EyeEm; Vsanandhakrishna/iStock/Getty Images Plus; Dennie Cody and Duangkamon Khattiya/Stockbyte; Laurie Noble/Photographer's Choice/Getty Images Plus; Marc Romanelli; xPACIFICA/The Image Bank/Getty Images Plus; Eye Ubiquitous/Universal Images Group; chee gin tan/E+; Nazir Azhari Bin Mohd Anis/EyeEm; Jan Kickinger/EyeEm; mustafagull/iStock/Getty Images Plus; acceptfoto/iStock/Getty Images Plus; Frank Krahmer/DigitalVision; boonchai wedmakawand/Moment; Photography by ZhangXun/Moment; **U8:** Moncherie/iStock/Getty Images Plus; sdominick/iStock/Getty Images Plus; izusek/E+; Mordolff/iStock/Getty Images Plus; Rubberball/Mike Kemp; ktaylorg/iStock/Getty Images Plus; Hill Street Studios/DigitalVision; Jose Luis Pelaez Inc/DigitalVision; Digital Vision/Photodisc; harpazo_hope/Moment Open; Dusty Pixel photography/Moment; Thomas Northcut/DigitalVision; BrianAJackson/iStock/Getty Images Plus; Elena Peremet/Moment; NoSystem images/E+; PeopleImages/E+; Hero Images; portishead1/E+; fergregory/iStock/Getty Images Plus; Compassionate Eye Foundation/Gary Burchell/DigitalVision; Hill Street Studio; Caiaimage/Sam Edwards; DragonImages/iStock/Getty Images Plus; **U9:** Heritage Images/Hulton Archive; Darius Dzinnik/500Px Plus; NurPhoto; Print Collector/Hulton Archive; Caiaimage/Martin Barraud; Scott Barbour/Getty Images Sport; Hero Images; Rick Gomez; Henn Photography/Cultura; AlexTurton/Moment; LUIS ACOSTA/AFP; JUAN MABROMATA; Pattanaphong Khuankaew/EyeEm; **U10:** DMITRY KOSTYUKOV/AFP Creative/Getty Images Plus; Smartshots International/Moment; Print Collector/Hulton Archive; Education Images/Universal Images Group; KTSDESIGN/SCIENCE PHOTO LIBRARY; VICTOR HABBICK VISIONS/SCIENCE PHOTO LIBRARY; LightFieldStudios/iStock/Getty Images Plus; YE AUNG THU; Huw Jones/Stone/Getty Images Plus; **U11:** J and J Productions/DigitalVision; Artur Didyk/iStock/Getty Images Plus; **U12:** Isaac Sánchez/iStock/Getty Images Plus.

The following photograph is sourced from another source.
U11: Courtesy of International Olympic Committee. .

Front cover photography by Pand P Studio/Shutterstock; Piotr Urakau/Shutterstock.

Illustrations

Fran and David Brylewski (Beehive Illustration); Amanda Enright (Advocate Art); Pablo Gallego (Beehive Illustration); Leo Trinidad (The Bright Agency); Dave Williams (The Bright Agency); Collaborate Agency; Wild Apple Design Ltd; Pipi Sposito (Advocate Art); Jake Mc Donald (The Bright Agency); Daniel Limon (Beehive Illustration).

Front cover illustrations by Alice Brereton; Amanda Enright; Pipi Sposito; Jhonny Nunez; Benedetta Capriotti; Leo Trinidad.

Audio and Design

Audio production by Ian Harker.
Song composition and production by Robert Lee at Dib Dib Dub Studios, UK.
Chant composition and production by AmyJo Doherty and Martin Spangle.

Design and typeset by Wild Apple Design Ltd
Cover design by Collaborate agency
Additional design layout emc design ltd

Official Cambridge Exam Preparation

Home Booklet 6

Stephanie Dimond-Bayir

Reading

1 **Draw lines from the words to the correct shape.**

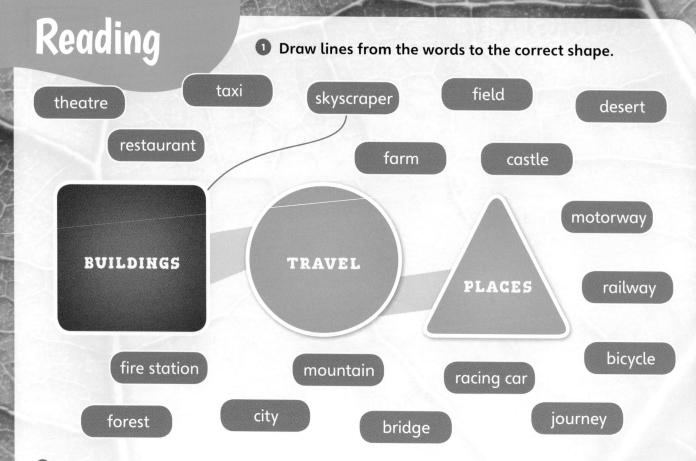

theatre   taxi   skyscraper   field   desert

restaurant   farm   castle

BUILDINGS   **TRAVEL**   **PLACES**   motorway

railway

fire station   mountain   racing car   bicycle

forest   city   bridge   journey

2 **Read and choose one word for each sentence.**

Example   This is very tall and you can see all over the city from the top.   *skyscraper*

1   You can pay the driver of this to take you somewhere.   _____

2   You can walk on this if you want to cross a river.   _____

3   You can go here to eat some delicious food.   _____

4   This has two wheels and is quicker than walking.   _____

Fun boost

Build your own town!

1 Find different boxes and pieces of cardboard.

2 Find some pictures and stick them onto the boxes or draw onto the card.

3 Paint or colour each building.

4 Put the buildings together to make your city.

Reading

it isn't

pizza

you

~~I can't~~

yoghurt

washing the dishes

kitchen

William is sending messages to his brother, Oliver. Read and complete the sentences with the words and phrases.

Hi, Oliver. I'm at the shop, but I can't find my money. Can you see it at home?

No, _I can't_ . I'm in the **1** _____ . Do you think it's here?

Maybe I left it there. Is it on the table?

No, **2** _____ . I can see some plates and a glass.
There's a **3** _____ for lunch, but there isn't any money.

OK. Can Mum look for it?

Mum's eating lunch and Dad's **4** _____ .

What about Jane?

She's getting some **5** _____ from the fridge.

OK, thanks. I'll come home and find it. See you later.

OK. See **6** _____ !

Fun boost

Read and write messages in English.

Can you read messages in English? Ask your friend to send you some questions on their phone or on a piece of paper. Read and reply. How quickly can you do it?

What's your favourite animal? Why?

It's a penguin, because they are funny when they walk. What's your favourite?

Reading

Find the words in the text and write them in the boxes.
Then find out where Sky is going on holiday.

I'm very excited about my holiday. I'm going to the beach and it should be very sunny. I've packed my sunglasses, but I won't need my umbrella. I'm taking everything in a backpack, because I don't need too many things. I'm putting in my trainers, because we will walk a lot and see different places. I've put in my camera, so I can take pictures. And I need to add a map on my phone so I know where I'm going on my journey!

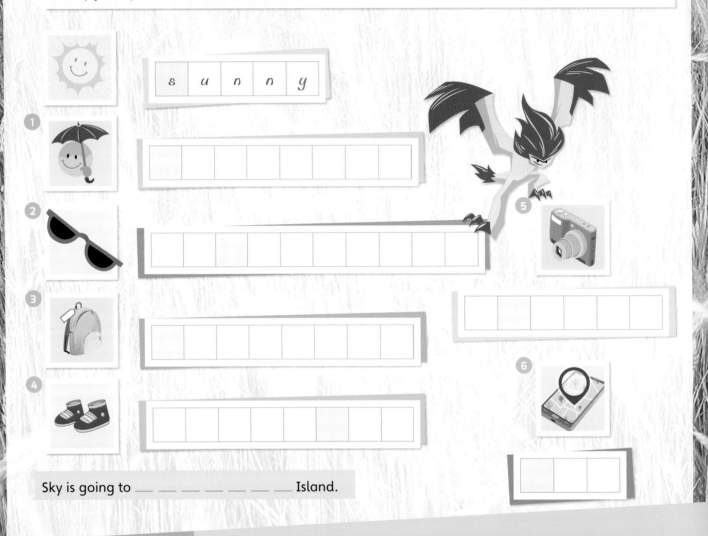

| s | u | n | n | y |

Sky is going to ___ ___ ___ ___ ___ Island.

Fun boost

Write a holiday list.

You are going on holiday with Sky. What are you going to pack in your suitcase? Write a list. Keep it for your real holiday!

Reading

1 **Read the story. Then answer the questions.**

Yesterday, I had an adventure. I decided to try different ways of travelling. First, I took a taxi, but it cost a lot of money and it was slow, because there was a lot of traffic on the motorway. Then I rode in a fire engine.

It was really fast, but dangerous. Then I tried the train. It didn't cost a lot, but the platform was crowded and there was a lot of noise. Next I tried riding a bicycle. It's very healthy because you use lots of energy, but I'm not very good at it and I got very hot. I finished my journey in a spaceship. I loved it. It was very comfortable and big, so next time I travel, I'm going to go by spaceship!

1 How many ways of travelling did Clunk try? _____

2 Which one did he like best? _____

2 **Write the correct word under each picture.**
Draw lines to show how Clunk describes them.

slow

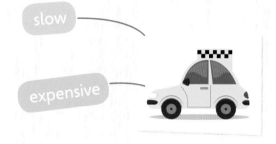

comfortable

expensive

hot

cheap

dangerous

taxi _____   _____

big

healthy

fast

_____   _____   _____

noisy

Fun boost

Think and say with your family.

Cover the picture. Can you remember four things with windows, three that can go on the road, two with four wheels and one that can fly?

A ... has got windows.

A ... can go on the road.

Reading

What kind of sandwich are you going to have? Read and draw lines to the correct instructions.

Cut two pieces of bread.

Cook the bread.

Put some chicken on top.

Cut an apple.

Put butter on one piece of bread.

Add some salad and tomato.

Add some honey.

Eat and enjoy!

Put the second piece of bread on top.

Put the salad into an oven.

Cut the sandwich in two.

Mix with some water.

Fun boost

What's your favourite strange sandwich?

Jo's favourite strange sandwich is jam, pizza and yoghurt. What will you put in your strange sandwich? Draw it and write the ingredients.

jam

pizza

yoghurt

Reading

1 Read and tick (✓) the correct pictures.

1 I've joined a new club. We meet every Wednesday at my school at four o'clock. It's really good fun.

2 It's called the International Club and we learn about different countries. We find out how many people live there and we draw the flags. These usually have primary colours like red and blue.

3 We draw pictures of the most important places and buildings. Last week, we drew skyscrapers, because we were learning about Tokyo in Japan.

4 We also learn about the animals that live in that place. For example, we saw a film about a butterfly garden in Japan. It was amazing.

5 I love going to the club. I've made lots of friends and at the end, we usually go to the park and play volleyball or have a picnic.

2 Find the words in task 1 and complete the text.

The time of the club is four **1** _____. We draw the **2** _____ of the country, so we need red and blue pencils. We find out about famous buildings like castles and **3** _____ . We also learn about the animals that live there, like the butterflies that live in the **4** _____ garden in Japan. After the club, we play **5** _____ in the park.

Fun boost

Find the flags!

1 Draw and colour the flag for your country.

2 Find out the flags of two other countries. Draw and colour them.

Reading & Writing

1 **Look at the picture. What do you think happened?**
Put the story in the correct order.

A Bill was unhappy. 'That's not very kind,' he said. 'Wait!
☐ Come back,' said the frogs. 'We want to say sorry!'
But Bill knew that they weren't telling the truth. So he
decided to play a trick. 'OK,' he said and he flew down very
close to them. The two frogs jumped in the air to try and
catch him. They jumped so high that they hit each other in
the air and fell down into the water. 'Ouch!' said the frogs.
'Sorry,' said Bill, 'but you shouldn't tell lies!'

B One day, Bill was near a pond. There were two frogs in the pond looking sad. 'Hello,' they said.
☐ 'Can you help us? We need some help finding our way across the pond.' Bill was frightened because
he knew that frogs eat bees. But the frogs said, 'Please help. We just want to find our way … come
down. We won't eat you.' So, Bill flew nearer because he was a very kind bee. When he got close,
one of the frogs opened its very big mouth and tried to catch him.

C Bill was a very friendly honey bee. He had black and yellow stripes and he flew from flower to
☐ flower collecting the nectar to make honey. As he was flying, he always sang a friendly buzz-buzz-
buzz song.

2 **Complete the text.**

Bill was a **0** _honey_ bee with black and yellow stripes. One day, he saw **1** _____ in the

pond. The frogs said they wanted him to **2** _____ them find their way. But they weren't very nice

because they tried to **3** _____ him. Bill wanted to play a **4** _____ on them. So he flew

near and the two frogs **5** _____ high, but they fell down instead.

Fun boost

Write sentences about animals.

Which kinds of animals can you find in a pond? Think of two animals. Write what they look like and
what they eat.

_____

_____

Reading & Writing

1 **Read and complete.**

Himmy and Kira have both been on a trip.

> I like doing lots of activities in new places. On this trip, it was quite hot. I went to museums. I saw the Great Wall and learnt some Chinese words.

> This trip was really fun. Some people only like going to hot places, but I like the snow and going to the mountains. So this was a wonderful place for me. I even learned to ski.

Who went to Norway? _____

Who went to China? _____

2 **Read the diary and write the missing words. Is it Himmy's or Kira's diary?**

Monday 18th February

I am having an amazing time here! We have walked up mountains and looked at the

ice lakes. I always take my **1** _____ and we buy hot drinks to keep us

warm. It is much colder than at home, so I am wearing my **2** _____ and

3 _____ , but I also have my **4** _____ with me because

it is very bright too! It's wonderful! I really want to come back again.

This is **5** _____ diary.

Fun boost

Make a Chinese lantern.

1 Fold some coloured paper in half and cut lines down the paper the size of a finger.

2 Don't cut to the edge of the paper.

3 Open the paper and bend it round to make a lantern shape.

4 Stick the edges together with glue.

5 Add a long piece of paper as a handle. You can also add different colour paper to the top and bottom, as in the photo.

Vocabulary: describing pictures

1 Write the words in the correct place.

blond   circle   curly   dark green   enormous   fair   gold
large   ~~light blue~~   ~~round~~   ~~short~~   silver   square   ~~straight~~

Size	Colour	Shape	Hair
short	light blue	round	straight

2 Look at the pictures. Put a circle around the correct words.

0 The boy is (standing) / sitting.

1 The girl is **holding / getting** a magazine.

2 The boy is looking **at / away from** his bag.

3 The girl is **putting / wearing** socks on her feet.

4 The boy **has got / is wearing** some trainers.

5 The girl is **laughing / smiling**.

3 Look at the pictures in Exercise 2. Choose the words to complete the sentences.

above   between   in   ~~on~~   under   without

0 The trainers are _____on_____ the seat.

1 The tennis racket is _____ the seat.

2 The magazine is _____ the girls' hands.

3 The bag is _____ the trainers.

4 The clock is _____ two pictures.

5 The girl _____ any shoes is on the sofa.

Part 1

Find the differences

www.cambridge.org/SageFlyers13

Asking questions

1 Complete the questions. Use the words from the box.

> Are   Do   Does   Has   Have   Is

0 _____Do_____ your parents like sports?

1 _____ the shop open at weekends?

2 _____ the houses got more than one floor?

3 _____ there any computers in Helen's classroom?

4 _____ Sarah's bedroom large?

5 _____ the park got any swings?

2 Match the questions with the answers.

0 Whose belt is this?

1 Which day do you play volleyball?

2 What time does chess club start?

3 How many cousins have you got?

4 How old is your sister?

5 Why do you like board games?

6 Where is the new toy shop?

A They're fun.

B I've got eight.

C On Thursdays.

D She's thirteen.

E In Kite Street.

F It's Mary's

G At quarter to four.

3 Write five questions you can ask your partner. Then answer their questions about you.

How many brothers do you have?   _I have two brothers._

What is your favourite sport?   _I like football._

1 _____

2 _____

3 _____

4 _____

5 _____

Part 2

Information Exchange

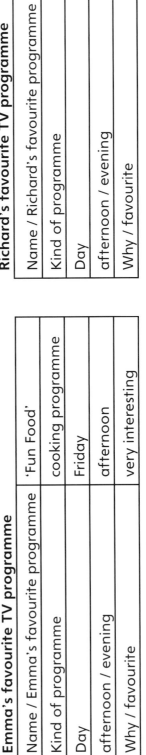

Emma's favourite TV programme

Name / Emma's favourite programme	'Fun Food'
Kind of programme	cooking programme
Day	Friday
afternoon / evening	afternoon
Why / favourite	very interesting

Richard's favourite TV programme

Name / Richard's favourite programme	?
Kind of programme	?
Day	?
afternoon / evening	?
Why / favourite	?

Information Exchange

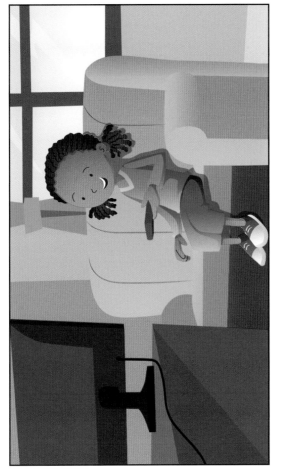

Richard's favourite TV programme

Name / Richard's favourite programme	'The Monkey Family'
Kind of programme	cartoon
Day	Monday
afternoon / evening	evening
Why / favourite	funny

Emma's favourite TV programme

Name / Emma's favourite programme	?
Kind of programme	?
Day	?
afternoon / evening	?
Why / favourite	?

Describing what's happening

1 Write words from both boxes to complete the sentences.

is isn't are aren't	a guitar player some swans ~~three trees~~ two people a group of people any clouds a roof

0 There _____ are _____ _____ three trees _____ in the park.

1 There _____ _____ with musical instruments on the stage.

2 There _____ _____ in the band on the stage.

3 There _____ _____ over the stage.

4 There _____ _____ in front of the stage.

5 There _____ _____ in the pond.

6 There _____ _____ in the sky.

2 Write sentences about the picture in Exercise 1. Use the words given.

0 Some people / listen / the music   _Some people are listening to the music._

1 A girl / play / the drum   _____

2 Three children / clap / to the music   _____

3 Two swans / swim / around the pond   _____

4 The girl / stand / on the stage   _____

Part 3

Picture story

The waterfall

Mum

Vicky

> Practise speaking about your home, your school, your family, your friends and the activities you like doing.

Now

1 Match the questions and answers. Complete the answers with one word.

❶ Where do you live?

❷ Who lives with you?

❸ Which school do you go to?

❹ How do you get to school?

❺ What do you like doing at weekends?

Ⓐ I _____ with my parents and brother.

Ⓑ I _____ there by car.

Ⓒ I _____ visiting my grandparents.

Ⓓ I _____ in London.

Ⓔ I _____ to High Road School.

The past

2 Answer the questions.

⓪ What did you have for breakfast this morning? — _I had cereal and some orange juice._

❶ What time did you get up this morning? — I got up _____.

❷ What did you do last weekend? — Last weekend I _____.

❸ What's the best film you've ever seen? — I think the best film _____.

❹ What were you wearing yesterday? — Yesterday I _____.

The future

3 Read the questions and write the answers. Then ask your partner the questions.

⓪ What are you going to do at the weekend? — _I'm going to play tennis._

❶ Where do you want to go on holiday next year? — _____

❷ What job do you want to do in the future? — _____

❸ What are you going to have for dinner tonight? — _____

Part 4

Answer the questions. Let's talk about your home.

Where do you live?

Which room do you like best in your home?

What do you like doing when you are at home?

Who lives twith you in your home?

Where do you usually have meals in your home?

Tell me about the home you want to have in the future.

Part 1

– 5 questions –

010 **Listen and draw lines. There is one example.**

George   Sophia   Holly   Sarah

Emma   Harry   Michael

Part 2
– 5 questions –

011 **Listen and write. There is one example.**

Children's Day at Great Lake

	Where:	Great Lake Water ___Park___
1	Date:	_____ June
2	Time sailing class starts:	_____
3	Name of sailing teacher:	Miss _____
4	What happens in the afternoon:	_____ by the lake
5	Don't forget to take:	a _____

Part 3
– 5 questions –

012 Daisy is talking about what she enjoys doing. Where does she do each thing?
Listen and write a letter in each box. There is one example.

cooking	B
playing volleyball	
making models	
playing a drum	
cycling	
chess	

A

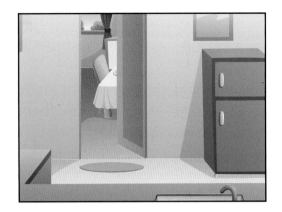

B

C

D

E

F

G

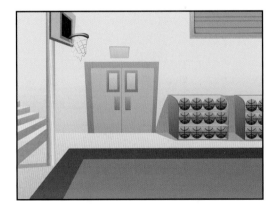

H

Part 4
– 5 questions –

013 **Listen and tick (✔) the box. There is one example.**

Where did Frank's parents buy a violin for him?

A ☐　　　　　B ☐　　　　　C ✓

1 Where does Frank practise his violin at home?

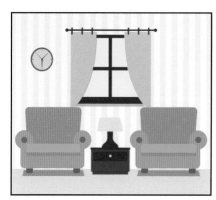

A ☐　　　　　B ☐　　　　　C ☐

2 What hurts when Frank plays the violin for a long time?

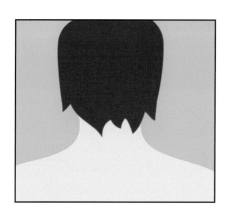

A ☐　　　　　B ☐　　　　　C ☐

53

3 What time is Frank's violin lesson today?

A ☐

B ☐

C ☐

4 Who does Frank like playing music with?

A ☐

B ☐

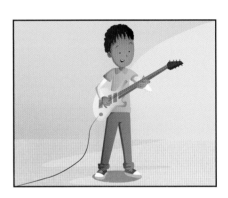

C ☐

5 Where will Frank's next concert be?

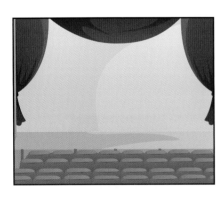

A ☐

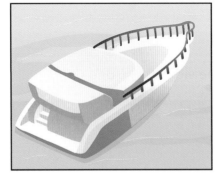

B ☐

C ☐

Part 5

– 5 questions –

014   Listen and colour and write. There is one example.

Part 1

– 10 questions –

Look and read. Choose the correct words and write them on the lines. There is one example.

projects   wood

plastic

maths

students

golf

channels

history

cartoons

snowboarding

card

volleyball

Teachers sometimes ask children to do these in class or for homework.   _projects_

1 These are people who go to classes at school, college or university. _____

2 There are lots of different kinds of these. You play music on them. _____

3 This is a winter sport that people usually do in the mountains. _____

4 Some warm clothes are made of this. It comes from sheep and other animals. _____

5 This subject teaches you about numbers and how to use them. _____

6 This is a sport that you play in teams. You have to hit the ball with your hands or arms over a net. _____

7 This is a kind of sports competition. The winner is the person who finishes first. _____

8 In this subject at school, you learn about things that happened in the past. _____

9 These are programmes on TV and they make children laugh. _____

10 Most bottles of water are made of this. _____

instruments   a race   wool

Part 2
– 5 questions –

Mum is talking to Holly about going swimming. What does Holly say?
Read the conversation and choose the best answer.
Write a letter (A-H) for each answer.
You do not need to use all the letters. There is one example.

Example

Mum:　Shall we go swimming this afternoon, Holly?

Holly:　＿＿D＿＿

Mum:　Which pool would you like to go to?

1　Holly:　＿＿＿＿＿＿

Mum:　We'll take the bus there and back.

2　Holly:　＿＿＿＿＿＿

Mum:　We'll need to leave the house at half past two to catch the bus.

3　Holly:　＿＿＿＿＿＿

Mum:　I don't know where your swimming costume is. Do you?

4　Holly:　＿＿＿＿＿＿

Mum:　What kind of snack would you like before we go?

5　Holly:　＿＿＿＿＿＿

Mum:　OK.

A	I think it's in the cupboard in my bedroom.
B	That means I've got lots of time to get ready.
C	All right, we'll have it at the pool.
D	Great idea! We haven't been to the pool for a long time. **(example)**
E	Good - I don't want to walk home after swimming.
F	Yes. I think the water will be warm today.
G	I'm quite hungry, so I'll have a sandwich, please.
H	The one at the sports centre. It's bigger than the one in the park.

Part 3
– 6 questions –

**Read the story. Choose a word from the box. Write the correct word next to numbers 1–5.
There is one example.**

Example				
together	early	straight	geography	next
uniforms	pockets	student	hurry	dark

Helen and Sarah are best friends. They do everything _together_ . They both go to Castle

Hill School, they both like playing basketball, and **(1)** _____ is their favourite subject at

school. They also both have **(2)** _____ , curly hair. But one big difference is that Helen is

tall and Sarah is short.

Last Thursday, the girls had basketball practice at lunchtime for the school team. They took off

their school **(3)** _____ and put on their sports clothes. After the game, they didn't have

a lot of time before their afternoon lessons started, so they had to **(4)** _____ . Sarah

picked up Helen's jumper and Helen picked up Sarah's – they were too hot to put them on.

The **(5)** _____ morning, they were both very surprised when they got dressed for school. Sarah's jumper was much too big for Helen – it looked like a dress – and Helen's jumper was much too small for Sarah. They took photos, and laughed at them all day!

(6) Now choose the best name for the story.

Tick one box.

Making friends   ☐

Time for new clothes   ☐

The wrong jumpers   ☐

Part 4

– 10 questions –

Read the text. Choose the right words and write them on the lines.

Could you be an astronaut?

| Example | You may be one of the many young people ___who___ want to travel into |
| 1 | space. So _____ you the right kind of person to be an astronaut? |

First, you must be very sure that this is the job you want because astronauts

2   have to study and work hard _____ many years before they are ready

to go into space. You must like and be good at science and engineering because

3   _____ astronauts have to study these subjects.

4   _____ you want to be an astronaut, you also have to be strong. You

5   can't get ill because there aren't _____ hospitals to go to!

Of course, astronauts should not be afraid of flying! Many of them have

6   _____ as pilots before they start learning to be astronauts.

7   To do this job, you also need to speak _____ than one language

8   because astronauts work with people _____ lots of different countries.

It is also important that astronauts are friendly and they should enjoy

9   _____ with other people. This is because the people in a spaceship have

10   to live and work together in such _____ small space.

Example	which	where	who
1	do	have	are
2	at	in	for
3	every	all	both
4	If	So	Or
5	some	any	a
6	worked	work	working
7	many	more	most
8	from	to	on
9	be	been	being
10	the	an	a

Part 5
– 7 questions –

Look at the picture and read the story. Write some words to complete the sentences about the story. You can use 1, 2, 3 or 4 words.

A place for skateboarding

Robert's dad worked in the park in their town. He looked after the park, and he grew all the flowers there. The flowers looked wonderful every summer, and hundreds of people visited the park to see them.

Robert and his friend Paul loved skateboarding around the park. But there was a problem. They had to be careful of the people who were walking on the paths, and when the park was busy, the boys couldn't go skateboarding there because it was too dangerous.

Last spring, Robert and his dad were talking. 'We need a special place for skateboarding in the park,' Robert said. Dad agreed, but added 'I'm sorry, Robert, the park hasn't got enough money for that.' 'We'll get the money!' said Robert.

Robert and Paul collected hundreds of old plastic cups from the park's café, and grew flowers in them. Robert's dad helped them. Then, every Saturday, they sold them to all the people who came to the park. The boys collected lots of money, but not enough.

Then, in July, a journalist wrote a story about Robert and his friend in their town's online newspaper, which she worked for. A very kind, rich businesswoman read the story, and thought it was fantastic. She gave the park enough money to build a brilliant place for skateboarding.

Examples

Robert's dad _____*grew*_____ flowers for the park.

A lot of people went to the park in the summer to __*see the flowers*__ .

Questions

1 Robert enjoyed skateboarding around the park with _____.

2 It was _____ to go skateboarding in the park when it was busy.

3 Robert's dad liked the idea of having a _____ skateboarding at the park.

4 Robert and his friend decided to make money by selling flowers in lots of _____
that they got from the park's café.

5 Every _____, the boys sold the flowers.

6 The _____ who wrote about the boys was from the town's online newspaper.

7 A businesswoman who was _____ gave some money for the skateboard park.

Part 6
– 5 questions –

Read the postcard and write the missing words. Write one word on each line.

	Hi Granny
Example	I'm having _____*a*_____ brilliant holiday. It's very cold here, and
1	_____ is lots of snow everywhere. We've just arrived at the hotel where
2	we _____ going to stay tonight. It's amazing because all the walls and
3	the roof are _____ of ice! The beds, chairs and tables are pieces of ice,
4	too. We have to _____ our coats inside because it's too cold if we take
	them off.
	I enjoyed my first trip on a plane. I could see the snow on the ground from the
5	window. It _____ really fun!
	Love from
	Emma

Part 7

Look at the three pictures. Write about this story. Write 20 or more words.

_____

_____

_____

_____

Part 1

Find the differences

Part 2

Information Exchange

Michael's best friend

Name	Harry
Where / meet	school
older / younger	older than Michael
Do together	play football
Why / like	very funny

Sophia's best friend

Name	?
Where / meet	?
older / younger	?
Do together	?
Why / like	?

Information Exchange

Sophia's best friend

Name	Sarah
Where / meet	Art Club
older / younger	younger
Do together	go camping
Why / like	very friendly

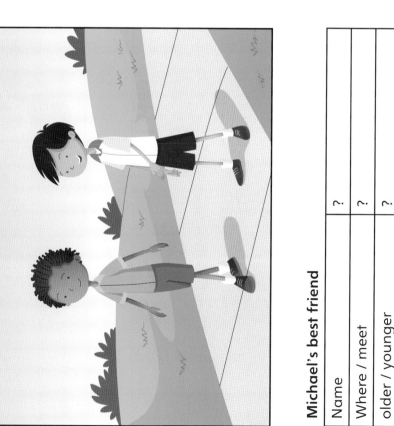

Michael's best friend

Name	?
Where / meet	?
older / younger	?
Do together	?
Why / like	?

Part 3

Picture story

The missing shoes

Julia

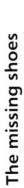
1

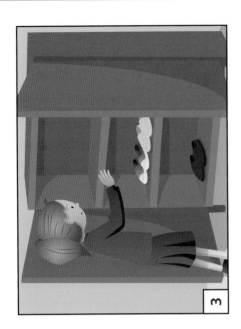
2

3

5

4

Part 4

Answer the questions.

Let's talk about school.

What's the name of your school?

Which subject do you like best?

What was your last lesson?

Who do you sit next to in your English lessons?

Where can you play in your break times?

Tell me about what you are going to do next week at school.

Acknowledgements

The authors and publishers acknowledge the following sources of copyright material and are grateful for the permissions granted. While every effort has been made, it has not always been possible to identify the sources of all the material used, or to trace all copyright holders. If any omissions are brought to our notice, we will be happy to include the appropriate acknowledgements on reprinting and in the next update to the digital edition, as applicable.

The authors and publishers would like to thank the following contributors:

Page make up, illustration and animations: QBS Learning

Squirrel character illustration and cover illustration: Leo Trinidad

Author: Frances Treloar

Audio production: DN and AE Strauss Ltd and James Miller

Editor: Alexandra Miller